Ernest Chausson

THE COMPOSER'S LIFE AND WORKS

Ernest Chausson

THE COMPOSER'S LIFE AND WORKS

BY

Jean-Pierre Barricelli & Leo Weinstein

Norman : University of Oklahoma Press

Library of Congress Catalog Card Number: 55–9627

Copyright 1955 by the University of Oklahoma Press
Publishing Division of the University
Composed and printed at Norman, Oklahoma, U.S.A.
by the University of Oklahoma Press
First edition

Introduction

Any biographer who sets himself the goal of re-creating a life must be considered presumptuous. He may possess documents covering every moment in the life of his subject, he may be a man of great knowledge and profound insights— with all these advantages he is still like a child looking through a kaleidoscope; every time the author feels that he has attained some sort of complete image, the slightest turn of the eyepiece reveals that what he had thought to be a definitive pattern was instead the tumbling view of partial perspective. The biographer turns the piece interminably until a larger pattern of permutations is at last visible and can be set down, but the triumph is more apparent than real, a bloodless conception that cannot retain the teeming reality of life.

A biography of Ernest Chausson is therefore less a re-creation than a suggestion. It does not have the posited strength of a construction, but rather the delicate, evocative quality of the less public feelings in our lives. It has this quality, this sense of incompleteness that Chausson's life mirrors, because of the paucity of surface drama in his public life. Beyond this and perhaps into the depths of his personal feelings, we meet with the strong sense of opposition that well-bred privacy interposes. Finally, there is unfortunately less documentation available than would satisfy the scholar and likewise too few personal reminiscenses to furnish that sense of "living with" that the biographer would like to convey.

Yet, despite, or because of, these difficulties—the problem of a life lived in a minor key, a reticent personality and the lack of complete documentation—the challenge of Chausson remains, the challenge of conveying in some poor measure the vision achieved by a man who searched for it desperately and with agonizing honesty.

In this biography we have attempted to let Chausson speak for himself whenever documentation permitted it. Where this applied (Chapter V, for example) we have effaced ourselves almost completely, merely filling in where gaps existed; elsewhere we had to step forward in order to supply background information, carry the thread of continuity or even speculate in the absence of positive evidence. When this was necessary, we have scrupulously endeavored to stick to facts as much as possible and not to slant these facts in favor of a particular interpretation.

We admit to being in sympathy with our subject—otherwise we would not have embarked on this venture; our attitude will inevitably be visible behind our words, for we are not automatons impassively recording the documents we have been fed. And yet we hope that our presentation has been such that the reader will be able to arrive at his own view of Chausson, an interpretation (such is the fate of the written word) which may, in fact, differ from our own.

Introduction

Only then can we claim to have transmitted at least a part of that great mystery—the life of a man.

We wish to express our sincere appreciation to the following for aid, advice, and services: Mme Etiennette Lerolle-Chausson, Mlle Annie Chausson, M. Gustave Samazeuilh, M. Paul Rouart, Professor Charles C. Cushing of the University of California at Berkeley, Professor Nathan Van Patten and Mr. Edward E. Colby of Stanford University, Stanford, California, Eleanor Foster and Germaine May of the French Broadcasting System, Peter Aby, Lawrence Margolis, James D. Ray, and Burton I. Wilner.

This work could not have been written without their kind help or without the generous aid of Fulbright grants to both of us.

J-P. B.
L. W.

August, 14, 1955

Contents

xi

Ernest Chausson

Illustrations

1

Ernest Chausson : *His Life*

1855-79

URING the 1850's Paris was beginning to take on the aspect which since has become so familiar to millions of tourists from every part of the world. Under the direction of Baron Haussmann the French capital was slowly being transformed from an essentially medieval city into a modern metropolis. Everywhere winding, narrow streets were giving way to wide boulevards, streaming in seemingly unending lines from the Place de l'Etoile.

A new era in French history was dawning. The times of barricades and class struggles, the bitter aftertaste of the Revolution and of the Restoration, the wild dreams of the romantics were over, at least for the time being. The failure of the poet Lamartine as head of the republican government in 1848 had forcefully symbolized the end of that period. The philosophy of the day was "realism," the future belonged to the bourgeoisie. After many years of social conflict—caused in part by the belated impact of the industrial revolution on France and resulting in the overthrow of the July Monarchy and of the Second Republic in turn—France could at last look forward to a period of political tranquillity, prosperity, and peace.

3

Ernest Chausson

For a decade Louis Napoleon fulfilled the high hopes which the nation had placed in him. He encouraged free enterprise and trade; inland markets were being opened for more intensive cultivation by the growing web of railroad lines spun from the hub of Paris and, save for the sporadic international forays of the Emperor, his conduct of affairs met with general approval; moreover, increasing prosperity had silenced social conflict by establishing a delicate balance among the classes.

The gradual loss of popularity suffered by the romantics had left a vacuum in the arts which was being filled by the more empirical-minded approach of Baudelaire, Flaubert, Guizot, and Courbet. In spite of the prevailing bad taste of the Second Empire, these artists succeeded in creating works marked by a just equilibrium of romantic and realistic features, thus duplicating, in a sense, the state of French society.

The only branch of art apparently unaffected by these new tendencies was the music of that period. While *Madame Bovary* and *Les Fleurs du Mal* suffered abuse from government and public alike, the French composers delighted their audiences with grand opera and operettas. Although a rich musical renaissance was taking place in Central Europe, French taste remained that of an elegant bourgeoisie, satisfied with the superficialities of an imported art—Italian song style and Austro-German virtuosity—and consequently chamber and symphonic works were almost completely neglected. The only outstanding composer of that time was Hector Berlioz, but he was unappreciated and known only to a small élite. Among the composers of "light music" only a few even deserve mention: Massé and Maillart, both writers of melodic and gracious music; Delibes, whose ballet scores reveal a personal and attractive composer; Ambroise Thomas, best known for his *Mignon*, who tried to lift comic opera to the level of grand opera; and Offenbach, whose tuneful melodies captivated Second Empire audiences. Over all these, however, Meyerbeer carried the day: adroit writing, *"coups de théâtre,"* vocal effects, violent action compensating for poor orchestration, lack of psychology, of depth, of taste, and of dramatic substance. The real milestone of this period was Charles Gounod's *Faust* (1859). Whatever objections may be raised against the dramatic interpretation of Goethe's work, this opera combined true, dignified, and fresh inspiration with new techniques and prepared the public for the musical renaissance in France which was to begin about a decade later.

ERNEST AMÉDÉE CHAUSSON was born in Paris on January 20, 1855.[1] His father, Prosper, was a wealthy building contractor who participated actively in Haussmann's renovation of Paris. Both Prosper and his wife, Stéphanie-Marcelline, born Levraux, seem to have been good, middle-class citizens without any particular artistic inclinations. Unfortunately, our documentation about Chausson's parents, his childhood, and his adolescent years is quite sparse. We are, therefore, necessarily limited in the range of our speculations regarding the early development of his personality. His parents had

[1] The date stated in all reference works at our disposal is January 21, 1855. The error is due to a misreading of Chausson's birth certificate which states: *"Aujourd'hui, 21 janvier 1855, nous a été présenté un enfant, né la veille . . ."* (emphasis ours); hence Chausson was born on the preceding day, i.e. January 20. We are indebted for this, and other, information to the late M. Guillaume Lerolle, the son of Henry Lerolle and nephew of Chausson.

previously lost two children and consequently took arduous measures to protect the safety of their third-born. Rather than send him to a public school, they hired a private tutor for his education, and apparently his mental formation was that of an overprotected child growing up in the company of adults. His tutor, Brethous-Lafargue, a highly cultured man, seems to have been the first to create in him an interest in the arts. Young Ernest read widely and beyond his scope of understanding, sketched, and eventually took piano lessons. But the absence of children of his age in the household instilled in him a reflective disposition: "This relative solitude, along with the reading of a few morbid books, caused me to acquire another fault: I was sad without quite knowing why but firmly convinced that I had the best reason in the world for it."[2]

Mme de Rayssac, whom he affectionately addressed as "godmother," exerted the greatest influence on the young Chausson. She was the wife of Saint-Cyr de Rayssac, a writer of delicate poetry who had fallen in love with her when she was still a young art student.[3] After her husband's death in 1874, Mme de Rayssac retired to live in a convent where her godson used to visit her frequently during his vacations.

Give my regards to the Mother Superior and, above all, do not tell her what I shall confess to you, for what I am meditating is almost a sacrilege. However, do not tremble and read on without fear. I hope my future sin will be forgiven. One of my best friends . . . is about to come and spend a few days at St. Quai. He is an admirable musician and a fine man, a Dutchman . . .

[2] August 4, 1876; to Mme de Rayssac.

[3] In an article devoted to the Rayssacs, in *La Vie littéraire,* II, Anatole France pays high tribute to her beauty, charm, and intelligence.

he is very religious, but his religion is rare and not wide-spread; I must tell you he is an Anabaptist. There still are a few. I take any responsibility in advance for his perfect courtesy towards the nuns and for his irreproachable behavior in the chapel, when he enters it, but will not the presence of a heretic scandalize these good sisters? It seems to me, however, that it would be difficult to leave him without food for two weeks. . . . If it is not necessary to go to mass on Sundays, it will be very easy for him to hide his anabaptism, and if it is absolutely necessary, he will keep quiet while there. . . .[4]

Their close association continued after Chausson, complying with the wishes of his father, had entered the law school at the University of Paris. Although he received his law degree in 1877, his studies apparently had not kindled much enthusiasm in him to practice the profession. On the other hand, he had never given up his love of literature, painting, and music. A decision had to be made at this time which would determine whether art for him was merely a pastime or whether he would henceforth devote his efforts to it alone. In his dilemma Chausson turned for advice to Mme de Rayssac: "Ever since my childhood I have believed that I would write music. Everybody counsels me against it. So I try painting and literature; everybody gives me a different advice."[5] Apparently he advanced a design which his godmother rejected out of hand; in any event his reply indicates this:

Your letter, my dear godmother, has had the effect you thought it would have. Through you I have seen more clearly within my-

[4] July 17, 1875.
[5] August 4, 1876.

Ernest Chausson

self. I have not forgotten anything, perhaps I have even forgotten too little. But I told you in the beginning that everything seemed complicated to me. I admit in a whisper . . . that I was profoundly amazed at myself: I did not think that I was so naïve, or so young; I assure you it is unbelievable. I did not reply at once, because I wanted to tell you the final outcome. The battle has been fought, but it was not completely decisive. . . . The crazy idea which motivated my last letter has now been irrevocably discarded. I had done so even before receiving your answer. As for the rest, all I can say today, by letter, is that your godson is neither prudent nor blasé but unbelievably inexperienced in certain matters. He is forming himself though, I assure you.[6]

Mme de Rayssac possessed the happy faculty of understanding her young godson *à demi-mot*. Their relationship was such that a mere suggestion sufficed to express an entire mood: "Do not be angry with me for talking with you as if we were still at Ouchy, in the evening, in your room, when you would say to me: 'My son, I hope it does not bore you to pose for me.' You, who understand what one says without words, you will understand why I write you in this way."[7]

Their letters deal with a great variety of subjects, ranging from artistic to personal problems, such as that of finding a suitable mate: "Yesterday I went to see Madame de M——, whom I found surrounded by a lady and four girls. The lady was Madame B——. I looked at the oldest of the girls, as you can imagine; I found her heavy, a bit talkative, ordinary in looks, stiff in her movements, briefly, everything that corresponded least to the description you had given me of her. It is

[6] Biarritz, 1878 (?).
[7] Munich, Englischer Hof, 1879.

8

true that your description may still be correct, for that young lady was not the daughter of Madame B—— but the governess of her children."[8]

After completing his law studies, Chausson continued to be torn by indecision regarding his future. For a while he tried his hand at various artistic endeavors: some sketching and oil painting; a literary project, *"Jacques,"* which he mentions to Mme de Rayssac without any further specification; and the composing of two songs.[9] This variety of talents and the relative temptation of economic ease and sufficient leisure to exercise these talents made the definite choice of a profession very difficult.

In 1879, Chausson took a trip to Munich, for he had become one of the early French admirers of Wagner. It is possible that the magnificence of the Wagnerian performances was in no small measure responsible for his ultimate decision to give up literature and painting in favor of music. This, however, meant that Chausson would have to face the handicap of a late start in what is perhaps the most abstract of all the arts. To master the technicalities of the musical script alone would mean long years of practice during which the means at his command would inevitably lag behind a full expression of his thoughts and feelings. Chausson's awareness of this problem lends a tragic note to his letter from Germany: "There is a phrase by Schumann which is terrible and which resounds in my ears like the trumpet of judgment day: 'One is only master of thought when one is master of form.'

[8] July 22, 1877.
[9] These songs, *Le petit sentier* and *Lilas, vos frissons,* can be found in the library of the Paris Conservatory.

Ernest Chausson

I feel more and more the truth of this thought, and it leaves me no repose. There are moments when I feel myself driven by a kind of feverish instinct, as if I had the presentiment of being unable to attain my goal or [of attaining it] too late."[10]

Nevertheless, a month later, Chausson enrolled in the Conservatory classes of Jules Massenet and César Franck: "I am glad of that somewhat unexpected decision, it will take much of my time, but . . . it was necessary. Franck is an admirable musician, somewhat mystical."

In his first year of study, Chausson concerned himself primarily with compositions for voice and for piano. Several of the songs contained in his Opus 2 were written during that period: *Nanny, La dernière feuille, Le Charme,* and *Les Papillons.* Their lyrical directness is such that, if we did not have evidence to the contrary, we might be tempted to ascribe to Chausson the facility of musical inventiveness of a Schubert. In his early piano works, Chausson did not fare equally well: the *Cinq fantaisies pour piano* (Opus 1) did not satisfy him, and he had the printing plates destroyed;[11] nor did a Sonatina and a Sonata in F minor meet his high standards. And neither one was published. "I have played my sonata for Franck and Massenet, who were very much pleased, especially Franck. Massenet made several objections. . . . As for the finale, its second phrase and a phrase from *Le Prophète* [by Meyerbeer] resemble each other like two drops of water. That surprised me all the more, since I never play that opera and hardly

[10] Munich, August, 1879; to Mme de Rayssac.

[11] One of the rare existing copies of this composition is contained in the Memorial Library of Music at Stanford University, Stanford, California. This library also possesses original mss. of *Cantique à l'Épouse, Chanson perpétuelle,* and *Le Temps des Lilas.*

ever happen to think of it. It is, however, quite true that the two phrases are identical."[12]

In the summer of 1880, Chausson revisited Germany to view once more the spectacular dramas of Richard Wagner. Even though he was obviously profoundly impressed by Wagner's art, Chausson's habitual critical outlook tempered his acclaim with sober afterthoughts brought on by his awareness of tradition:

I have heard *Tristan,* which is marvelous; I don't know any other work which possesses such intenseness of feeling. As pure music it is splendid and of the highest order; as a way of understanding the musical drama it is a revolution. Gluck already had a presentiment of it, but since then people have hardly thought about it. Wagner has taken up his work, has enlarged and transformed it, and created a new art which will inevitably overturn the old molds of the opera. . . .

The performance of *Iphigénie en Aulide* which I heard the morning after my arrival is not as Gluck wrote it. Wagner made some changes in it which were unnecessary, and some of them seem very unfortunate to me.

. . . . . All in all, I do not easily approve of these retouchings in a work of genius, even if done by a man of genius such as Wagner, and I would have preferred to hear simply Gluck's score as it was written.[13]

Late in 1880, Chausson, realizing that he could not continue working with two teachers as fundamentally different as Massenet and Franck, decided to study henceforth with the latter exclusively. This was perhaps the most far-reaching

[12] October 10, 1880; to Mme de Rayssac.
[13] Munich, July 22, 1880; to Mme de Rayssac.

decision in Chausson's musical career, because in Franck's circle he acquired not only the craft of a skilled musician but infinitely more—a code of life which replied to his deep-seated but as yet unexpressed aspirations, and the happy experience of a man who discovers that his cherished ideals are shared by others.

1880-83

BETWEEN Chausson's birth and the time he began his musical studies, France had undergone many profound changes caused primarily by the French defeat in the War of 1870. Although the nation had made an amazing recovery and even though prosperity had returned, the scars of defeat were deep and lasting. The artists, the most sensitive barometer of an intellectual climate, expressed these changes faithfully in their works; it seemed as if a new perspective— harsher, more penetrating, and at the same time more brutal —had ripped off the last layer of velvet which the artists of the 1850's had draped over bare reality. In literature Emile Zola had established the naturalist novel, based on minute ob- servation and almost scientific detachment broken only occa- sionally by its founder's sense of social justice or the veiled compassion of a Maupassant. Just as this new trend tended to upset the delicate equilibrium between reality and imagina- tion achieved by the preceding generation, so the grievances which led to the Commune uprising in 1871 had put an end to social harmony.

This time French music too had been stirred from its long slumber, but what took place was not so much a revolution as a slow transformation from the mediocrity which had prevailed during the preceding twenty years. This transformation had actually begun in the 1860's, when such composers as Camille Saint-Saëns, Jules Massenet, Georges Bizet, Gabriel Fauré, and César Franck first attracted some attention. After the War of 1870 these men took up their work with renewed energy. To be sure, the French concert-going public continued to acclaim operatic productions of slight value; nevertheless, the war had created an interest in German music and, if Wagner was as yet opposed by French patriots, Beethoven was constantly gaining new admirers; furthermore, this fresh crop of composers and the presence of first-rate orchestras offered new possibilities: the technical study of music and the education of the public.

Among the factors contributing to the eventual renaissance of French music, three require special mention: the founding of the Société Nationale de Musique, the steadily increasing influence of Wagner in the realm of the lyrical drama, and the teaching activities of César Franck.

The Société Nationale de Musique was founded in 1871 by Camille Saint-Saëns and Romain Bussine, a professor of voice at the Conservatory. Its statute reads in part: "The aim of the Society is to aid the production and popularization of all serious musical works, whether published or unpublished, of French composers; to encourage and bring to light, so far as it is in its power, all musical endeavor, whatever form it may take, on condition that there is evidence of high artistic aspiration on the part of the author.... It is in brotherly love, with complete forgetfulness of self and with the firm intention of aiding one another as much as they can, that the members of the Society will cooperate, each in his own sphere of activity, in the study and performance of works they shall be called upon to select and to interpret."

This society, which has upheld these noble principles to the present day, created new opportunities theretofore unattainable for young composers of serious music; in fact, "M. Romain Rolland does not hesitate to call the *Société Nationale* 'the cradle and the sanctuary of French art.' 'All that has been great in French music from 1870 to 1900,' he says, 'has come by way of it. Without it the greater part of the works which are the honor of our music not only would not have been performed, but perhaps would not even have been written.' And he draws from the program records of the performance of important compositions by Franck, Saint-Saëns, d'Indy, Chabrier, Lalo, Bruneau, Chausson, Debussy, Dukas, Lekeu, Magnard and Ravel."[1]

In the midst of these developments a crisis intervened which shook at the roots of French music: Wagnerism.

Since the time of the Second Empire, Wagner had found enthusiastic admirers in Paris and it was not their fault that *Tannhäuser* . . . had been unsuccessful at the Opéra [in 1861]. His conduct during the war, when he had not hesitated to trample on the defeated nation, removed from him its sympathies for a while. But for a while only, for from 1873 on, Pasdeloup . . . began a most tenacious propaganda campaign in his favor. Not discouraged by such tumultuous incidents as took place in 1874 and 1876, he finally gained a true success for Wagner's music by means of selections from *Lohengrin,* in April and May, 1879. . . . In 1885, Lamoureux succeeded in having an all-Wagner program

[1] Daniel G. Mason, *Contemporary Composers,* 162f.

applauded and, on May 3, 1887, a full Wagnerian opera was performed at the Eden Theater, the first since the failure of *Tannhäuser*—again *Lohengrin*. This performance was an apotheosis, and on the next day Paris had a new idol, Wagner. His name was on everybody's lips. . . . This infatuation approached the limits of frenzy. People went in groups from Paris to Bayreuth in order to attend performances of the masterpieces of the Master in the place which he had chosen for them and they returned home with transfigured faces. It was gravely discussed whether it was permissible and proper to play Wagner on a French stage. Finally the question was answered affirmatively and the modern mystery plays were given at the Opéra or at the Opéra-Comique, changed into "temples" for the occasion . . . in an atmosphere of self-communion and exaltation which is difficult to describe to any one who did not experience it. Scenes took place which until then had been the mark of religious fanaticism. There were sudden conversions, outbursts of Dionysian furor against the "unbelievers"; the faithful of the Wagnerian religion did not tolerate the slightest scepticism.

Without doubt, for many pure and ardent souls the cult of Wagner was a means of escaping from the frightful atmosphere of vulgarity and low taste which reigned at that moment in our literature and our politics. . . . Wagnerism was thus in many ways a protest of the uncoercible idealism of our race against the sad moral and intellectual diet to which circumstances condemned them.[2]

By enlarging the use and scope of polyphony, Wagnerism had thrown the education of young musicians into confusion: thenceforth, a composer faced the dilemma of either imitating Wagner or fighting a hopeless struggle against him, for Wagner had realized his ideal so completely that no other

[2] Louis Reynaud, *L'influence allemande en France au XVIIIe et au XIXe siècle,* 274f.

form of originality seemed possible. At any rate, falling back on the old, stereotyped grand opera was out of the question.

César Franck showed a way out of this predicament by demonstrating that philosophico-symbolical expression was not necessarily the ultimate possibility in music. Although Franck admired Wagner, he urged his students to eschew total absorption in the theater and the inevitable imitation of the German model in favor of a more promising program: the return to the tradition of the masters and the serious education of the public to symphonic and chamber works. During his lifetime Franck attracted relatively few students; he had the reputation of being an excellent organist but a worthless teacher, and at the Conservatory he was held in such low esteem that only the organ class was entrusted to his charge—the composition courses went to other composers. But the students who gathered around him at the Conservatory or at the famous organ loft in the Sainte-Clotilde Church soon discovered that *"le Père Franck"* was not only a lovable man and a great composer but a teacher of the rarest kind as well.

The Franckists were a free but homogeneous school. What united them was a common purpose combined with the ideals which their teacher proposed to them. The most important disciples of the great master, those who came to be known as *"la bande à Franck,"* included Vincent d'Indy, Henri Duparc, Pierre de Bréville, Charles Bordes, Guy Ropartz, and Ernest Chausson.[3]

[3] Vincent d'Indy (1851–1931), foremost of Franck's disciples. As a teacher he influenced the following generation; with Charles Bordes founded the Schola Cantorum, a free conservatory opposed to official teaching, which

Ernest Chausson

For all these young men ... the author of the *Béatitudes* was not simply a professor of counterpoint. He offered them the example of his own life, the evidence of his saintliness: the word is not too strong. He preached to them not by words but by his actions. He turned them away from egoism, from the superstition of success. He taught them modesty, disinterestedness, self-forgetfulness, contempt for popular applause, respect for the great masters, the cult of sincerity. . . .

The influence through which César Franck gained the hearts and minds of his students never turned into tyranny. No teacher was ever more respectful of his students' personalities; he did not permit them to copy his manner; he looked for any germs of originality in order to cultivate them. One cannot think without surprise at the variety of talents he formed. Thus Ernest Chausson

---

also published many ancient and forgotten works. His copious production includes: *Chant de la Cloche,* a lyrical legend for orchestra, soli, and choruses; *Wallenstein,* a symphonic trilogy; *Fervaal* and *l'Etranger,* lyrical dramas; *Istar,* a symphonic suite; *Sauge fleurie,* a symphonic poem; *Tableaux de Voyage* for piano; *Symphonie sur un Thème montagnard français,* symphonies, and chamber music.

Henri Duparc (1848–1933): Illness interrupted his production prematurely; left few works, among which *Lénore,* a symphonic poem, and about a dozen songs have established him among the finest French song writers.

Pierre de Bréville (1861–1949): He wrote several symphonic compositions and a lyrical drama, *Eros vainqueur.*

Charles Bordes (1863–1909): He gave up composing in order to teach; was co-founder of the Schola Cantorum; founded also the Société des Chanteurs de Saint-Gervais to revive the purity of religious music. Bordes composed principally songs, some chamber and orchestral music on Basque motives; left an almost completed drama, *Les trois vagues.*

Guy Ropartz (born 1864): His works carry the imprint of his native Brittany; was appointed director of the Conservatory at Nancy; wrote symphonies, chamber music, songs, and a drama, *Le Pays.*

Among the remaining students of Franck we find Alexis de Castillon (1838–73), Guillaume Lekeu (1870–94), Camille Benoît (1851–1923), Arthur Coquard (1846–1910), Augusta Holmès (1847–1903), and Sylvio Lazzari (born 1860).

Ernest Chausson as a child

did not know the shackles of a school or the burden of imitation. In his first works he was himself and expressed without restraint, effortlessly, the reveries of his youth.[4]

Aside from their contributions to symphonic and chamber music, the Franckists played an important role in the development of the French art song, the *"mélodie."*[5] In its close fusion of song, poetry, and instrumental commentary, the *mélodie* constitutes in many ways the French counterpart to the German lied. Although Berlioz and Fauré had written songs in this manner prior to 1870, the *mélodie* received its greatest impetus after the Franco-Prussian War and has remained one of the finest French musical traditions to the present day. "This small, intimate form was cultivated for the initiate, and it has remained little known outside of France, beyond a few of the more popular examples of Debussy, Fauré, Reynaldo Hahn, and possibly Chausson. Ignorance, however, is not entirely due to neglect. It must be admitted that the charm of the French mélodie is not easily discernible, though on acquaintance one is increasingly aware of an overpowering sweetness of effect, an exquisite subtlety, compared with which Schubert, in the eyes of certain French critics, appears all too innocent and guileless."[6]

The impression seems to persist that the Franck group

[4] André Hallays, *"Le Roi Arthus," Revue de Paris,* Vol VI (December 15, 1903), 846–58.

[5] The French art song is not only referred to as *"mélodie"* but also at times as "lied," although this last term is properly applied only to songs which have their roots in German folk music or which have been affected by it.

[6] Edward Locskpeiser, "The French Song in the Nineteenth Century," *The Musical Quarterly,* Vol. XXVI (1940), 192.

kept aloof from the other composers who contributed to the renaissance of French music. This was not at all the case. Franck himself maintained excellent relations with most of his colleagues. To be sure, Massenet would occasionally be somewhat upset by the carelessness of his fellow-teacher at the Conservatory. In his unworldly ways Franck would some-times schedule his organ class at the same hour as Massenet's composition course, and it was not an uncommon occurrence to see Franck, wondering why his students were not arriving, stick his head into Massenet's classroom to look for them.[7] Nevertheless, the two men had the highest respect for each other. Moreover, being active in the Société Nationale, the Franckists were necessarily in close touch with their con-temporaries. Thus Franck shared the presidency of the Na-tionale with Camille Saint-Saëns for a number of years; Emmanuel Chabrier became an intimate friend of many Franckists, especially of D'Indy and Chausson, and even Georges Bizet used to drop in once in a while on Franck's organ class. On one of these occasions, "the day of the *première* of *Carmen,* Bizet offered three seats to Franck's class; . . . lots were drawn and one of them fell to d'Indy, who could attend this memorable performance.

---

[7] Another reminder of Franck's absent-mindedness has been preserved in the souvenirs of Chausson's family. Franck often used to drop in for a chat while the Chaussons were still having breakfast. While talking in his exuberant manner, he would take Mme Chausson's hand in his. As she could not continue her meal and disliked eating cold food, her husband, in order to free her, hit upon the idea of placing a sugar bowl in Franck's hand. While Mme Chausson eagerly returned to her breakfast, the great master would tenderly caress the bowl, which has remained in the souvenirs of the family as *"le sucrier du Père Franck."*

His Life: 1880–83

"During the first intermission d'Indy and his friends were strolling along the rue Favart. They notice Georges Bizet, walking nervously with a friend. They greet him; they expess their vivid admiration. The composer shakes hands with them, saying dejectedly: 'My dear fellows, those are the first nice words I have heard and I do believe they will also be the last.' "[8]

A special place in this brief review must be reserved for Gabriel Fauré, who independently pursued a course similar to that of Franck. As France's leading writer of art songs and a most important composer of chamber music, Fauré had outlined a path which offered much to a sensitive young musician; beyond that, one can easily detect a sort of temperamental kinship in the combination of personal lyricism and refinement of expression which pervades the music of both Fauré and Chausson. It is no great wonder, therefore, that Chausson loved and admired few musicians more than Fauré. Because the two men saw each other frequently, correspondence between them is scarce, but whenever Chausson mentions Fauré, he speaks of him in the warmest and most affectionate terms.

Ambroise Thomas and Charles Gounod were the only important French composers of that period who felt little sympathy for Franck. The former, as director of the Conservatory, deprived him of a promotion to professor of composition, while the latter, then the dean of French music, sharply disapproved of his musical innovations. "The affirmation of incompetence pushed to dogmatic lengths, " reportedly was Gounod's judgment of Franck's Symphony in D minor, a

[8] Léon Vallas, *Vincent d'Indy*, I, 201 f.

condemnation which continued to prevail for some fifteen years, covering the efforts of Franck and his students with such abuse as to make a fair hearing well-nigh impossible.

For Ernest Chausson, Franck's teaching proved to be a revelation. The musical affinities of the two men were undoubtedly deepened by temperamental resemblances: their strong sense of reserve, their modesty, and their religious beliefs. In later years Chausson, the disciple, expressed his admiration for the lofty spirit of Franck's musical thought: "The works of Franck are not made to be enjoyed after dinner in the midst of people who talk and dilate with emotion only at a *ritenuto*. To understand them, as all works of art worthy of this name, it is necessary to have a sense of beauty and an elevated taste. His music no more belongs to what is called in society 'the artistic accomplishments' than the fugues of Bach, the quartets of Beethoven, the tragedies of Aeschylus, or the poem of Dante."[9]

Along with the other faithfuls of the great master, Chausson was quick to respond to the enthusiasm which Franck inspired in his students. In 1881, encouraged by the progress he was making in his work, Chausson decided to compete for the *Prix de Rome*.[10] Apparently, he entered the competition hastily and under unfavorable circumstances, for no mention of the *Prix de Rome* can be found in his letters prior to the contest; nor was the nature of his entries likely

[9] *Le Passant*, 1891.

[10] The *Prix de Rome* is an award for study in Rome, bestowed annually by the Institut de France on the winner of candidates from the composition classes of the Conservatory. In 1881 the award went to Alfred Bruneau. Chausson's entries included *l'Arabe* for male choir with tenor solo and orchestral accompaniment, and a Fugue for Four Voices on a theme by Saint-Saëns.

to sway the judges. The letter which he wrote to Mme de Rayssac after learning of his failure in the contest contains neither excuses nor complaints—just strong disappointment with himself; however, he expressed his determination not to become discouraged. A few months later he has recovered well enough to attempt the composition of a trio, his first chamber work:

> You are undoubtedly expecting to receive a letter of lamentations, as every year. Not so at all. I do not groan any more; I do not get impatient when my work is not proceeding as I would like it to (and that happens often, even most frequently). I do my best, I read it over, I erase (oh! very much) and I begin over again with enraged gentleness. . . .
>
> Do not think for a moment after reading this that I am falling into indifference or, worse than that, into dilettantism: nothing would be farther from the truth. I detest the word and what it stands for. But I feel an enormous desire in me to do something to the best of my ability. . . .
>
> I feel vague things, impossible to define as yet. And I am putting myself into a state of grace in order to invite them to come closer. As soon as I have seized them, I assure you, I shall not let them go.
>
> Let me tell you about last night. Ah, my dear friend, how truly delightful it was. I was busy, alone, writing some wretched transitions for the Trio . . . my window was open, the night completely calm; and, behold! a nightingale begins to sing in a tree nearby. There is nothing astonishing in that, is there? It happens every day. But just then, I don't know why, the voice of that bird filled me with emotion. How many things I felt and understood in those few moments! Don't make fun of me (I know very well that you don't dream of it), that bird was full of profound thoughts. He certainly knew the great secret; he had waited until all the noise

had quieted down, until all the intruders, those who do not understand the mystery of the night, had gone to sleep, in order to come here to sing his song at the shore while the distant swirling of the dam was discreetly accompanying him. I don't know of anything which has ever given me an impression of innocence and conscious resignation like that voice. But that too is what it means to live according to nature! The pretty little being, inoffensive, grateful, ephemeral and joyful! He gallantly refutes Schopenhauer and Pascal; the Gospels mean more to him. He looks at the stars and sings. Is that not the supreme philosophy?

I am telling you all this very badly; you can probably imagine it for yourself: imagine these not unusual things; a not very starry but silent night, trees, a river, a man of the end of the nineteenth century, having read, like everybody else, many books, alone, uncertain, impressionable, and a bird singing. That is all.[11]

This is no longer the young man who drew Mme de Rayssac's disapprobation for his wild ideas. Above all, there is a tendency towards simplicity: no more searching for effects, no more elegant bantering; all this has given way to understatements, mere indications of feelings.

On April 8, 1882, the Trio was performed at a concert of the Société Nationale. The music critics paid no attention to the work of the unknown composer. They were not particularly interested in chamber music, and very few of them attended the performances of the "radical" Société Nationale. But Chausson, encouraged by Franck's praise, had already set out on his first instrumental attempt. True to Wagnerian tradition he chose a legendary subject, that of Viviane, the beautiful maiden who, having learned the art from the en-

[11] Undated letter; probably written in 1881.

chanter Merlin, puts him to sleep when he wants to flee from her embrace.

As had been the case with the Trio, the first performance of *Viviane*, on March 31, 1883, aroused no particular interest; a repeat performance, on March 30, 1884, however, resulted in a few favorable reactions. Nevertheless, not satisfied with the work, Chausson revised it extensively, and it was not played again until 1888, at which time the critics applauded it.

Aside from being Chausson's first symphonic composition, *Viviane* marks another important event in his life. The work is dedicated to Mademoiselle Jeanne Escudier, whom he married in 1883. They had been introduced by the sculptor Alfred Lenoir, a close friend of Henry and Madeleine Lerolle, Jeanne's sister; as Jeanne was an accomplished pianist, it is likely that their common love of music served as an effective catalyst in their courtship. The marriage was a very happy one, for Chausson found in his wife an ideal companion: she not only raised the five children which she bore him, but proved to be an elegant hostess and an affectionate wife as well. Chausson, for his part, was a devoted and faithful husband who fully appreciated the rare qualities of his wife: "What a child I still was at eighteen! I realize that from a certain point of view I have changed very much and that change is due exclusively to the influence of Jeanne on me. I have become less complicated. With my life based on a true and deep feeling, I find fewer difficulties in the things around me."[12]

Marriage did not interfere with Chausson's composing; on the contrary, his wife's interest in music gave him the

[12] Paris, November 19, 1884; to Mme de Rayssac.

encouragement he needed. He still preferred to compose in quiet places and therefore left Paris whenever possible. On these trips the entire family usually accompanied him. Once arrived at their destination, he would find himself a calm place and compose there in perfect solitude. In time Chausson came to adopt more regular working habits: he would begin his day with a cold shower; then he would warm up with some piano playing, frequently from Bach's *Well-Tempered Clavichord;* when he was running into difficulties with his work, he would go for long walks in the country.

Chausson's marital happiness was temporarily interrupted by a call to military service. During his brief career in the artillery, Chausson expressed his distress in a letter to his good friend Paul Poujaud, an ardent music lover: "I despise it [the military life], not because of philanthropy but simply because one does not have a moment of freedom."[13]

Chausson returned to civilian life with renewed energy. During most of 1884 he centered his attention on the lyrical drama. Two projects occupied him, *Hélène* and a work on the death of Hercules, but the former gave him so much trouble that he decided to drop the latter:

Besides the great men, there are thousands of little ants which grind away, sweating conscientiously, without receiving any appreciation; what they do is of little consequence; it does not change anything and yet they cannot do otherwise. Why the deuce am I one of those beasts? It is no use saying that facility is not a quality, which is perfectly true; it is also true that a certain degree of pain indicates that will power is forcing nature. . . . It is only a

[13] Le Mans (Sarthe department), 1884.

step from there to wondering whether it would not be better not to write anything. But that is exactly where my lack of logic becomes apparent. I am speaking to you, my dear friend, with complete frankness, because I am sure you will not make fun of me. I am guided neither by vanity nor by false modesty; that fools nobody, not even oneself. I know very well that I can succeed one day or another in writing a musical work that would be interesting to a few curious people, but between that and a true work of art there is a whole world. How is it that I can't stop writing? I have tried to; I can't; there is in me then something like an organic function that is not doing its work; I become completely unbearable. The strangest thing is that, in spite of everything I have just told you, . . . I am working as if, at the present moment, I thought quite differently. But once the verve is gone, I rage upon seeing how far what I have written is from what I wanted to write, from what I thought I heard in my mind. And the next morning I work just the same.[14]

One reason for his difficulties can be found in his awareness of the tyranny which Wagner exerted over the lyrical drama. It was apparently during his work on *Hélène* that Chausson first began to realize the dangers of Wagnerism. As late as 1883, upon learning of Wagner's death, he had exclaimed: "And now Wagner is dead! But he has written Tristan!"[15] When Chausson began work on *Hélène,* he had assured his godmother: "I have done all I could in order to avoid being too Wagnerian."[16] But now, seeing Wagner's shadow everywhere, he writes angrily: "Add to that [the other difficulties in his work] the red specter of Wagner that

[14] Villiers-sur-Mer, 1884; to Poujaud.
[15] February, 1883; to Mme de Rayssac.
[16] August 16, 1884.

does not let go of me. I reach the point of detesting him. Then I look through his pages, trying to find hidden vices in him and I find them."[17]

This was not his last encounter with the giant from Bayreuth, for Chausson believed that he was best gifted to write for the stage. Although he produced fine dramatic works, it is now generally agreed that he excelled especially in symphonic music and in the more intimate atmosphere of chamber works and song. Yet Chausson's belief regarding his talents is by no means unique in the history of art: was it not Molière's greatest ambition to be a tragic actor?

[17] Villiers-sur-Mer, 1884; to Poujaud.

1883-89

AFTER completing his formal studies with Franck in 1883, Chausson traveled so frequently and so extensively that, if we were to draw a map of his journeys, it would resemble a wheel with numerous spokes emanating from Paris, most of them pointing to the South. Anxious to escape from the noisy distractions of the capital, he sought the peaceful countryside whenever circumstances permitted: ". . . nature is not playful; neither the sky nor the fields talk to me of *soirées* or dinners in town. . . . I am all alone all day long in a little abandoned village; I hear only the distant chant of a cuckoo and the surging of life in the growing wheat. How beautiful this calmness is. I see everything in a new light; I feel myself becoming better."[1]

This delight in nature marks a definite romantic trend in Chausson; yet any sentiment he may have held in common with the romantics of the earlier nineteenth century was strongly tempered by a number of factors: a solid bourgeois background which he never denied, the emphasis on structure and form which Franck had impressed on him, the criticism

---

[1] Chavigny, via Chambourg (Indre-et-Loire department), 1885; to Mme de Rayssac.

which had been heaped on the excesses of romanticism, and his habit of severe self-criticism: "This eternal swooning before one tree or two trees which form a bouquet, or three trees which form the beginning of a forest, irritates me in the long run. Not that my taste for nature is diminishing, but I am seeking something other than the object itself. If I were a landscape painter, I would think differently; as I am not and don't even paint with oils any more, I admire especially those things which evoke ideas in me."[2]

Even if it had not been for these influences, Chausson's personality alone would probably have kept him from becoming a romantic, because any kind of confessional outpouring was repugnant to his nature. This trait had already been in evidence during his early correspondence with Mme de Rayssac: "Words are very imperfect signs for conveying what one means; ... I prefer to let you guess my thoughts between the lines, since one hesitates most of all to express those feelings which are most intimate."[3] His music reflects in many ways the same *"état d'âme"*; rarely overpowering in sentiment, it is yet evocative enought to suggest to the sensitive listener its hidden tonal emotions, those "thoughts between the lines."

French critics have labeled this aspect of Chausson *"pudeur,"* a sense of modesty suggestive of shame. The term is somewhat misleading, because it inevitably carries with it a vague connotation of effeminacy. Chausson's *"pudeur,"* if such it must be called, is more than an inbred sense of reserve and propriety; it is the assertion of masculine strength, of

[2] Crémault, June, 1886; to Poujaud.
[3] July 22, 1877; to Mme de Rayssac.

the determination to cope unaided and unpitied with his personal problems. If Chausson frequently stopped short of "confessional" expression, he was swayed not only by personal but by artistic scruples as well. He was an extremely conscious artist, conscious of the tradition behind him and of the means at his disposal, a trait of character that prompted a fear of falling into the use of clichés and a consequent advance rejection or careful re-examination of a great many ideas. What Chausson did share with the romantics was lyricism. And it is in this very fusion of his lyrical inspiration, critical faculties, and attention to structure that we find the genius of the man.

Again like the romantics (and yet how unlike them), Chausson was haunted by the problem of death, or perhaps rather by a Pascalian awareness of the brevity of life, which crops up in his letters from time to time:

How everything has changed! And how many have died during these ten years! When I think of what I have accomplished since, I have for an instant the real sensation of the rapidity of time. Ten years! and so few works. Do I still have ten years left to live? Then, for a moment I feel fear, not of death, but of dying without having done what I was called to do. And I work and I curse Paris and the vain worldly activities which prevent us from thinking about the only things worth thinking about, which often prevent us from seeing the only friends we truly love.[4]

Chausson feared death only insofar as it might prevent him from accomplishing his task; in every other respect, he looked beyond the time of life with the same confidence as his

[4] Chavigny, via Chambourg (Indre-et-Loire department), 1885; to Mme de Rayssac.

teacher: "Death is our goal, the most real moment of our known existence; now, if you take this point of view, the only true one, how all things around us, things to which we often give the largest part of ourselves, suddenly change in importance! How badly led, badly understood and badly lived our life seems to us! Since that is our fatal goal and since death, as I am firmly convinced, is not an end but a beginning or a beginning again, why live as if we did not know what is awaiting us tomorrow perhaps or in a few years?"[5]

Aside from these ominous forebodings, Chausson was enjoying the happy life of a young artist who, on his own for the first time, sees the world around him with new eyes. The slightest stimulus sufficed to lead him to musical projects, to new emotional searchings. One day, in a barber chair, he was facing a woodcut of Raphael visiting Leonardo da Vinci while the latter was at work on the "Mona Lisa." "I thought ... it would be fun to write the music which, it is claimed, Mona Lisa heard while Leonardo da Vinci was doing her portrait. Be assured in advance that nothing is further from my mind than a pastiche of old music. I simply (!) want to explain in my own way the mystical smile of Mona Lisa and why, in appearance at least, she seems to be so unimpressed by those beautiful mountains which surround her and by that delightful little river behind her."[6]

He intended to write this work as a triple quartet for strings, wind instruments, and voices. "I shall certainly add to this a bass, which would give me a tredecetto, a brand-new

---

[5] Quoted by Charles Oulmont, *Musique de l'Amour,* 110f.
[6] from the Château de Crémault, Bonneuil-Matours (Vienne department), 1886; to Poujaud.

form as the name indicates." However, the composition never materialized; nor did a number of projected symphonic poems, which were to include *La Nuit, Printemps* (after Botticelli), and *Chant de la Terre*. It is not impossible that he finally decided to combine his various ideas into a single work.

I have not spoken to you about the countryside, because I have hardly looked at it while admiring and *feeling* it very much. I even ought to be grateful to it, for it has just furnished me with an idea that I had been vaguely seeking for a long time. You know my antipathy towards descriptive music. At the same time I felt incapable of writing pure music like Bach and Haydn. Therefore I had to find something else. I have found it. It only remains to be seen whether I shall have the power within me of expressing what I am feeling. As long as I am only thinking of it, I am full of confidence; once I have a pencil in my hand, I feel like a very small boy. Think of the *Fontaine aux Lianes* by Leconte de Lisle. Take away its exotic aspect (Indian flowers) and the semi-dramatic aspect (the dead man with eyes wide open) and you will be able to make yourself an approximate idea of the poem in question. . . . I want a poem that I compose alone in my head and of which I only give a general impression to the public; I want, moreover, to remain absolutely musical, so much so that those listeners who would be unable to follow me completely, can be sufficiently satisfied by its musical aspect. There is no description in it, no hint of a story; only feelings.[7]

Chausson first intended to entitle his work *Dans les Bois;* when Camille Benoît proposed calling it *Solitude,* the composer combined the two into *Solitude dans les Bois.* It was

[7] Crémault, June, 1886; to Poujaud.

performed on December 12, 1886, but Chausson was dissatisfied with the work and he destroyed it, this time, unlike his Opus 1, without bothering to have it printed. "Good heavens!" exclaimed one who was present at the performance, "how disconsolate that solitude was! Was it a pain that bitter which the poet-musician felt upon contact with nature?"[8]

Of all the plans conceived during that period of intense intellectual and artistic germination, the most far-reaching one was contained in a manuscript which Chausson sent to Poujaud in 1886. It was the first draft of the libretto for a projected opera, *Le Roi Arthus*. Although his difficulties with *Hélène* had awakened some misgivings about Wagner in him, Chausson still followed in the German's footsteps by writing his own text and choosing his subject from legendary sources: the Lancelot episode combined with the death of King Arthur. From the very beginning Chausson was plagued by the apprehension that his story might resemble *Tristan* too closely.

The few months which Chausson used to spend in Paris were filled with activities of a different nature. His spacious home,[9] decorated by his brother-in-law Henry Lerolle, became the meeting place of the intellectual élite of his time. The list of his guests reads like a "Who's Who" of the late nineteenth century: Albert Besnard, Eugène Carrière, Odilon Redon, Édouard Manet, Auguste Renoir, Edgar Degas, and Auguste

[8] Julien Tiersot, "Ernest Chausson," *Guide Musical,* Vol XLV (June 25, 1899), 503–504.

[9] At 22, Boulevard de Courcelles. At present the house is divided into several offices. A plaque, indicating that Chausson lived there, was placed on it during a ceremony commemorating the fiftieth anniversary of his death, in 1950.

Chausson's home at 22 Boulevard de Courcelles, Paris. The photograph, taken in 1950, shows the commemorative plaque (just above the bench) placed there during the observance of the fiftieth anniversary of the composer's death.

Rodin represented the painters and sculptors; among the poets and writers we find: Stéphane Mallarmé, Henri de Régnier, André Gide, Colette, Gérard d'Houville, Camille Mauclair, Maurice Bouchor, and Henri Gauthier-Villars. Most numerous, of course, were the composers: César Franck, Emmanuel Chabrier, Henri Duparc, Vincent d'Indy, Gabriel Fauré, Camille Chevillard, Sylvio Lazzari, Raymond Bonheur, Guy Ropartz, Albéric Magnard, Charles Koechlin, Gustave Samazeuilh, and Erik Satie; and among the performers: Eugène Ysaÿe, Jacques Thibaud, Armand Parent, and Alfred Cortot.

It is a monumental loss that among Chausson's guests there was not a Marcel Proust who could have immortalized the brilliant gatherings at the Boulevard de Courcelles. Thus many a historical soiree, at which one of the guests would unveil a new work, has vanished with those who were present. Henry Lerolle, in a letter to Chausson, preserved at least one of these evenings for us:

> Yesterday we had our little meeting. Present were d'Indy, the hero of the evening, Poujaud, Benoît, Bordes, Debussy, the Maurice Denis. . . . I had asked Debussy to bring along *Pelléas,* but upon arriving he told me that he had not brought it, because that would amount to too much music.
>
> So, after dinner d'Indy went to work. He told us in his most bizarre style the subject of his third act, then he played and sang it for us like a little girl reciting her lesson.
>
> After *Fervaal* [d'Indy's opera] we talked, some sincere compliments—then at midnight the Denis left. . . . Benoît wanted to go home with Poujaud who preferred to stay and meanwhile Debussy was tinkling on the piano seemingly thinking of something else— then "Now, come on"—"But I have nothing to play"—I find

Pelléas in his brief case—and Debussy becomes enthusiastic, d'Indy turns the pages, and Poujaud looks very much impressed.[10]

Chausson's home also served as a place of reunion for César Franck and his disciples. The latter felt very much hurt by the contempt with which their teacher was treated in official circles, and, in 1884, Chausson had set out on a determined campaign designed to obtain admission into the Legion of Honor for the composer of the *Béatitudes*. To that end two all-Franck concerts were arranged at Chausson's home, but they failed to produce the desired results. When the ribbon of the Legion of Honor was finally bestowed on Franck, it was due not so much to the recognition of his merit as to some skillful wirepulling on the part of Albert Cahn, one of Franck's lesser-known pupils. Cahn whispered a few well-chosen words into the ear of the painter Bonnat, who was then painting a portrait of the President of the French Republic, and as a result Franck was appointed chevalier of the Legion of Honor on August 4, 1885. To celebrate that occasion, his students gave a banquet in his honor at which they presented him with a baton inscribed with their names.

Those who *premièred* their works before the prominent audience at Chausson's receptions were not necessarily always established artists. The host delighted in extending this opportunity to newcomers, for throughout his life Chausson distinguished himself as an enthusiastic champion of young musicians. His election as secretary of the Société Nationale de Musique, an office he was sharing with D'Indy, enabled him even more to use his influence on their behalf. It is a credit

[10] October 19, 1893; Lerolle to Chausson.

not only to his generosity but also to the sureness of his taste that he encouraged the early efforts of such men as Albéric Magnard, Paul Dukas, Gustave Samazeuilh, Maurice Ravel, and, not least of all, Claude Debussy.

The two men had been introduced by a common friend, Raymond Bonheur, a fellow-student of Debussy's at the Conservatory.[11] Debussy took an immediate liking to Chausson, and in time a deep and lasting friendship united the two men. This is all the more surprising in view of their difference in temperament and the fact that Debussy had left Franck's class with a sneer. When times grew difficult for Debussy, Chausson welcomed him to his home and helped to provide him with jobs (such as playing piano versions of Wagnerian operas in Paris society) in order to supplement Debussy's meager income.[12] It was Chausson, too, who paid for the first deluxe editions of Debussy's *Poèmes de Baudelaire* and *La Damoiselle élue*. Debussy never forgot Chausson's kindness; in fact, it has been said that in his harsh musical criticisms Debussy spared only two composers: Chausson and D'Indy.

During 1888 and 1889, Chausson evolved—not miracu-

---

[11] Debussy's *Après-midi d'un Faune* is dedicated to Bonheur; so is Chausson's *La Légende de Sainte-Cécile*.

[12] That Debussy did not always enjoy these tasks is evident from a letter by Lerolle to Chausson, dated *"Lundi gras,* 1894": "Saturday, private performance by Debussy of *Parsifal;* it went off very well, even though a few people felt that one could not hear the words clearly enough. You know how he pronounces when he sings and we were lucky when he did not say tra-ra-ta-ta. Poor Debussy was at the end of his strength, he was playing and singing with such animation that I thought he was going to drop. In short, Debussy does that like others carry baggage in order to earn some money."

lously, but painfully—from a writer of small-scale works to the composer of the Symphony in B-flat Major and of the Concert for piano, violin, and string quartet. Actually, his production in 1887 and 1888 had been small: mostly songs, including settings of Gautier's *La Caravane* and Richepin's *Chansons de Miarka.* He had also been at work on a song cycle of Bouchor's *Poème de l'Amour et de la Mer;* this, up to then his most ambitious vocal effort, was a sign of increasing self-confidence. One reason for this comparatively slim output was his preoccupation with *Le Roi Arthus,* his opera which caused him more trouble than any other of his works. Not only did Chausson have to fight the influence of Wagner every step of the way, but his overpowering sense of self-criticism kept his ideas from asserting themselves: "Odilon Redon was indeed right when he said that inspiration is a 'state of grace.' If one cannot enter that state by oneself, one can at least prepare to receive 'grace' whenever it may come. That is what I am endeavoring to do. . . . There is above all that frightful Wagner who is blocking all my paths."[13]

This battle with the German giant quickly crushed a momentary note of hope:

I am beginning to have a little confidence, not in what I am doing but in what I shall do with this drama [*Arthus*]. . . . How light-hearted I feel, my dear friend. It infuriates me, but that changes nothing. My feelings are more stable, fortunately. . . . I am entangled in a lot of confused ideas, which run into one another, jostle each other, one chasing away the other, and sometimes returning a little while later. I understand nothing about anything. I feel in myself the most contradictory things. . . . With

[13] Crémault, June, 1888; to Poujaud.

me that lasts for a long time; it only gets worse. I have yet a few little lights left and I feel so many winds blowing in all directions which threaten to extinguish them.[14]

Living at a time when eccentricity was a mark of artistic distinction, men such as Franck and Chausson surprise us by their utter lack of "bohemianism." Although their efforts met with but little appreciation, they did not heap abuse on those who sneered at them. These men did not claim any special privileges for being artists; nor did they believe that, in order to create, an artist could not be a good family man. They had no quarrel with their government or with their religion; they did not issue manifestoes or engage in verbal squabbles. Their only reply to critical attacks was more work and silence, the silence of the strong.

The Franckists' abhorrence of publicity, coupled with lives which lacked exterior excitement, was a decided disadvantage in bringing their works to the attention of a public which was unaccustomed to hearing serious music. But the blame for the indifference with which their early efforts were met falls partly upon the group itself: some reasonable publicity and a less aristocratic attitude—in short, better public relations—might have brought improved results. Chausson was even more handicapped by his reluctance to offer his works to a publisher for fear that it might be said he had taken advantage of his good connections in Paris society or that he might be depriving a needy colleague of a chance to have something published. On the rare occasions when he did go to see a publisher, he met with little encouragement. Up to this time Hamelle had published most of his works,

[14] Crémault, 1888; to Poujaud.

but now the publisher was holding up the printing of *La Caravane* and of *Hymne védique* by asking Chausson to pay a subsidy of five hundred francs. The usually so gentle composer rose in anger and stormed out of the office, leaving the publisher aghast.

Towards the end of 1888, Chausson finished the composition of incidental music for Shakespeare's *Tempest*. The occasion was a performance of the comedy in Bouchor's translation at the Petit Théâtre des Marionettes. Chausson must have taken great pains with these short pieces, for he had a boundless admiration for Shakespeare.[15] André Hallays, in his brief but excellent study of Chausson's music, remarks concerning this work: ". . . in the French sense of the word, its accent was not romantic, but that does not at all mean that, on the other hand, it is not Shakespearian."

The critics, however, did not take to it. As late as 1892, Henry Frène, writing in *Progrès Artistique,* exclaimed: "As for . . . the selections from the *Tempest* by M. Chausson, we admit our inability to follow these gentlemen in their musical fantasies." And M. Frène's colleague Charles A. Garnier of the *Revue de l'Evolution* added: "We shall say nothing about a song by M. de Bréville and an entr'acte by M. Ernest Chausson. They are amateurs who consider music as an agreeable pastime; it would be unkind to discourage them."

M. Garnier was not the last to call Chausson an amateur. Had he been able to observe the composer at work, he would perhaps have wondered why a man should struggle so desperately for an "agreeable pastime."

[15] Writing to Poujaud in 1884, Chausson added this postscript: "I consider you a fortunate man for being able to read Shakespeare in the original."

1889-93

IN 1889, Ernest Chausson was thirty-four and as yet he had not written a major work. Of his two symphonic poems, *Viviane,* it is true, had aroused a few favorable comments when an altered version had been played on January 29, 1888, at the Concert Lamoureux, but the approving voices had come from friendly critics; the other tone poem, *Solitude dans les Bois,* had so displeased him that he had destroyed it.

When at last, upon the urging of his brother-in-law Henry Lerolle, Chausson agreed to begin work on a symphony, he realized that this was going to be the important test which would tell whether he was merely a gifted writer of songs and of shorter works or whether he would be able to take his place among the masters of music.

As usual, when Chausson was ready to compose, he left Paris, this time for Olhaberrieta, a villa located at Cibourre near Saint-Jean de Luz. He did not expect the job to be an easy one, but not even in his most pessimistic moments had he imagined how much suffering it would require to bring his symphony into being. At first the work offered no more than the difficulties to which Chausson was accustomed. The first movement, which he had probably turned over in his mind before leaving Paris, was therefore sketched in relatively short time. But the andante! The torture was about to begin.

I had told you that I would not write you again until my andante would leave me in peace. Well, I am not through with it yet. Since this morning, however, I have seen a little light and I believe I can finish sketching it this week. But, believe me, it was hard work. And I am not convinced that the middle section is as good as the beginning; quite on the contrary. You rascal, it is you who got me started on this confounded symphony. If you had been here, I would have said much nonsense to you. But, since you are far away, I want you at least to have a share in it. I am dedicating it to you. So much the worse for you if it is not better. Yet, I have done all I could. I am speaking of it as if it were finished. I do so, because I dare not think of the finale which I shall never get out of the way; I still have quite a few nice days of torture ahead of me. That is especially due to the nature of ideas which do not lend themselves to symphonic developments. Nothing can be done about it. After the heavy, sad, and long andante I am afraid to begin at once a finale which is lively but not very much so, being also somber and weighty. . . . I have a scherzo for the middle section that would not fit badly, I think, but I have not yet decided on the general aspect I want to give to the piece. I would not want a classical scherzo. It would have to go with the whole work and that is quite difficult with the rhythm of the scherzo. Of course, I can take another one, but which one? However, I believe that I shall finally find it. The reason I am in favor of the scherzo is also to a great extent my fear of beginning that terrible finale.[1]

Henry Lerolle must have been somewhat taken aback when he received the following letter a few days later:

[1] Olhaberrieta, Tuesday, 1889; to Lerolle

His Life: 1889-93

Your confounded symphony is throwing me into a fine state indeed. I have at last finished the andante, or nearly so, but by a violent means. I went through a torture that you cannot imagine in order to write the middle section with a phrase I did not like but whose general aspect fitted the movement. The chance of a modulation made me finish short. That can be taken care of. I took pleasure in thinking that I had finished. Then I played the whole thing over and I saw very clearly that the middle section was not only detestable, which does not amaze me, but also perfectly useless. I shall simply have to cut it out, make a skillful bridge, if I can, and smoothe out the ending. Still, I am sure that I shall get through with it. Just the same, you will have made me spend a terrible time. And it is not finished. Pray that I find something good for the finale; otherwise I shall insult you by letters, by telegrams, any way I can.

I am quite egoistic, am I not? I am speaking only about myself. You must not hold it against me. I am brutish. As long as I have not finished the sketch of the finale, I cannot be considered a responsible man.[2]

The crisis was approaching. With two movements completed, there was no turning back; yet the agony of composing the finale proved almost too much for Chausson. Ideas had never come easily to him, but this time the struggle evinced from him a cry of despair.

Dear friend, I am bewitched. All those stories about spells and witchcraft . . . are true, for I have certainly been subjected to a fate of that kind, or else it has come by itself and gotten hold of me. It is not a question of gritting my teeth; rage, despair, all that is merely childish babbling compared with the frenetic state in which I am. It is truly raving madness. There is a reason for it: Just

[2] Olhaberrieta, Saturday morning, 1889.

43

think, since being here I have been working like a slave and I am stuck at one measure! I have tried to stop, impossible. I return to my paper as to a vice. To do anything else, also impossible. I cannot think and think only of that one measure. So I loathe it; I hurl insults at myself, I hit myself with my fists. As you can imagine, that helps a lot. Most horrible of all, what I am about to write is very good. I don't tell you that often about my music; this time I sincerely believe that it is good. No doubt about it, it is even too good for me; I had a lucky beginning and now I find myself afloat without being able to continue, unwilling to give up, a prey of frenzy. I play over incessantly what I have written, always hoping that a good inspiration will enable me to get by the fatal measure, and it is always the same thing, and I begin again and stop once more. Imagine, I stopped just a moment ago. It was for the twentieth time today. It is like that every day. It will be like that again tomorrow. I no longer dare get up in the morning, thinking of the frightful day I am going to spend. . . . In my lucid moments I try to recognize my malady. And I have found it, all of a sudden. It comes from my songs. Ah! I detest them now and I hope never to write any again. All of them bad, except Hébé perhaps and fifteen measures of Nanny. The cream of music! harmonic clashes that are perhaps pretty but which intoxicate, enervate and lead to impotence! . . . You were right about Debussy. That is not what he should write. And yet, it is pretty, I still like it, but because it is the music of someone else. Oh no! that is not the kind of music I would like to write. Look up de Bréville. Try to make him understand that he is running into an open abyss. Cite me as an example! Tell him about the rotten state (let us hope it is temporary) in which I am for having written songs which some of my friends have found pleasing. . . .

Now, don't make fun of me but advise me. I need an idea; I have it on the tip of my tongue, I am almost thinking it or rather I suspect it. Impossible to write it. That ought to be a known

malady. Send me drugs, advice but no consolation. I absolutely
have to lie down. I assure you I cannot possibly continue leading
this sort of life.

Adieu, I am going to begin all over again. If anything comes
of it, I shall tell you in a post-script. If there were any use in curs-
ing, but no, that does no good. I am not going to curse. I remember
you don't like that.

Your friend,
ERNEST CHAUSSON

P.S. I thought for a moment I had found it, but no, that is not yet
it. However, at the last moment I perceive a feeble light, I'll get
back to it after dinner or tomorrow morning. I am worn out.[3]

The desperate search for inspiration blocked any further
efforts to compose, and Chausson, at wit's end, permitted
himself a respite from the tremendous nervous tension. He
rented a car and visited Roncevaux, the site of the *Song of
Roland.* The contemplation of past glories helped him re-
cover from his frenetic state, which had probably been partly
due to overwork. Upon his return to Olhaberrieta we find
him "up to his neck" in Mozart's *Magic Flute:*

How delightful, how exquisite it is; you could not ask for anything fresher or more original. It seems to me as if I am reading
that score for the first time. A sign of age. As we grow older we
have a greater liking for youthfulness. Just take a look at Gounod
and see how soft he has grown, artistically speaking. Now he is
pressing the score of *Don Juan* to his heart, because he knows that
it contains ideas, warmth, life, that is to say things which he does
not have or has no longer. Could it be that perchance I too have
reached that stage? That would be precociousness. Without flatter-

[3] Olhaberrieta, 1889; to Poujaud.

ing myself, I hope to have yet a few years ahead of me. Don't think that I have fallen into writing so-called simple music. No, that is finished for good. That was a delightful moment which could not last. It is not in that direction that we must look. The only thing which is truly ours and which our terrible ancestors have been unable to take away from us is our manner of understanding and feeling. That can always vary with each man. Let us then put as much as possible of ourselves into our works. That is what I am endeavoring to do. And I continue to play without fear and with delight entire acts of the *Flute*.[4]

The crisis is overcome, work on the symphony progresses more smoothly, Chausson's letters are calmer; the composition occupies less space in them. A note to Lerolle from Arras mentions some difficulties with the first two movements. Finally, in 1890, a letter to Poujaud from Ayzac casually reveals the completion of the work.

I have told you little about my work this year. The reason is that I pass so often and so quickly through alternate states of rage, gaiety, enthusiasm and despair that I find it preferable not to cast light on these shameful nuisances. Recounting them grants them too much importance. And, when my friends answer me, it always happens that my state of mind has changed and, if they speak of my "good work" at the moment when I am pulling my hair out, I howl and accomplish even less. . . .

The Symphony is finally finished except for a few light retouchings. . . . Send me news about Fauré's health. Don't you think that some possibility must be found to let him spend a quiet winter outside of Paris? Consider the most fantastic means of arranging that and think also of what I am not saying and answer me. In these matters nothing is impossible, provided there is a will to do something. . . .

[4] Olhaberrieta, 1889; to Poujaud.

His Life: 1889–93

The first performance of the Symphony in B flat Major took place on April 18, 1891, at a concert of the Société Nationale in Paris, with Chausson himself conducting. As he walked to the conductor's podium, he could be sure that the majority of the audience present was sympathetically inclined, but it was equally certain that many critics would automatically condemn the work in advance, because it had been produced by a disciple of Franck. What a happy occasion it would have been if Chausson's old teacher could have been present at this performance; but, alas, *"le Père Franck"* had died the previous year without receiving any due recognition for his own works or for the school he had founded, and thenceforth it was up to his students—to D'Indy, Chausson, Duparc, de Bréville, Ropartz, and Bordes—to carry on Franck's work.

The performance was greeted with enthusiastic applause; but, if there was any rejoicing among the Franckists, it was premature, for, on the whole, the Symphony did not arouse much interest among the critics; yet, a few of them, who had previously been hostile to Chausson's works, were outspoken in their approval. Thus the *Figaro* contained this reaction: "M. Chausson, whom we had known until now as an imponderable musician, has been transformed and appears this time clear and straight-forward in his ideas." Even more significant was the judgment of A. Ernst, who wrote in the *Siècle Progrès Libéral:* "I was all the more glad to hear and to applaud this symphony as it has happened many times that I did not at all enjoy the musical productions of the young composer, too indecisive until now in my opinion; today I believe I saw a personality asserting itself, more conscious, clearer and also more colorful. At any rate, it is a significant work, great and beautiful in appearance which does honor to our school."

Although these few critics had been conquered by the beauty of the Symphony, most of the others were not much impressed. The *Gazette de France* carried these lines: "Divided into three movements, it begins with a somewhat somber prelude, followed by a brief cello solo in a religious mood; next comes a harmonic ensemble of the violins nicely followed by a *crescendo;* then . . . but here it becomes so confused that I understood nothing. In the second movement I point out very disagreeable dissonances and a very sonorous finale. If M. Chausson will but moderate himself, he will give us nice things, for he is not short of wind. But he really had too many friends in the hall; their ovations were noisy and immoderate." While the foregoing is at least somewhat objective—negative, perhaps, only due to the writer's inability to appreciate the work on first hearing—others were frankly hostile; for example, the critic of *Le Monde Musical:* "We are so unfortunate as to be profane and we declare quite modestly that it is impossible for us to analyze his works, because we found nothing in them. The symphony of M. Chausson offers perhaps some interest in its musical texture and in its orchestration which seems to hold its own."

After all the suffering which had gone into the writing of Chausson's symphony, he must have felt some disappointment at the lack of interest shown in this work, but if he did, he never expressed it. He was no doubt still mindful of the lines which he had written some time ago to his friend Vincent d'Indy: "When I think of our teacher Franck who devotes all his days to giving piano lessons, cannot work for himself except for two months in the summer, writes then masterpieces which no conductor accepts, does not pronounce a single bitter word, does not let a word of rebellion escape, I am truly amazed if any one dares complain."[5]

Although the first performance of the Symphony was far from successful, Chausson had nevertheless proved to himself that he was capable of creating works on a large scale. The effort which this composition had required did not leave him exhausted. It seems as if a sudden illumination had come over him, an illumination caused by the simultaneous maturing of all his faculties. Even while working on the Symphony, Chausson had been sketching a most original chamber composition: the Concert[6] for piano, violin, and string quartet. Apparently, the work advanced fairly smoothly at first, for only rarely is there a reference to it in his letters; but then, as he had done with the Symphony, he covers it with invectives: "I have only made progress on the *Concert,*" he writes from Civray in 1891. "As long as that animal is not finished and copied, I feel that I cannot be calm." Again the composer was gravely dissatisfied with what he had produced. Worn out by constant effort, he felt that he had fallen short of his ideal. "Another failure" was Chausson's gloomy judgment of the work.

[5] Quoted in *Feuilleton du Journal des Débats,* February 16, 1900.

[6] This work is often listed as "Concerto," which is a misinterpretation of its title. Chausson did not intend to write a double concerto (which, in fact, is implied by those who call it a "concerto"), but a work in which the solo instruments blend in with the ensemble; thus the term "concerto" fits here no more than it would fit a piano quintet. As far as we have been able to ascertain, this is the only work of its kind.

Ernest Chausson

After completing the Concert, Chausson, in dire need of rest, took a trip to Italy. He had not been in that country for some time and found, to his disappointment, that there a too rapid "progress" had wrought many changes.

... Fortunately there is still the sea. I say still, for it too will not always remain. There has already been talk of erecting along it casinos in more or less Moorish style. I really believe I am getting old. ... I am no longer in the swing of things. The conquests of civilization do not at all fill me with enthusiasm. The other day I saw an enormous balloon advertisement. As if it was not enough to cover the walls of even beautiful monuments. Now the sky is covered. Villiers de l'Isle-Adam had foreseen it, alas, only too well.

In Lyon, near Fourvières, I read this macabre but not banal sign in a shop window: "Mortuary cloak of greatly religious character, easy to put on, even for the most belated funeral."

I hear the sound of the sea and I see the stars. That at least is good.[7]

In Florence, Chausson encountered Richard Wagner's wife and son. He relates this meeting in a letter to Poujaud from near-by San Domenico di Fiesole, his favorite domicile in Italy:

Just imagine, I had dinner with Mme Wagner and Siegfried the day before yesterday. In Florence, unexpectedly. Siegfried is not very amusing. He has come here to write a comic opera and Florence does not please him. The beer is not good here. That may well be so. He has an unpleasant way of speaking about modern art. His musical opinions, except for the founder of the house, are rather like those of Pougin, and Bouguereau himself is not

[7] Nice, 1891; to Poujaud.

more severe on those unfortunate painters who are unwilling to paint in his manner or that of Raphael. . . .[8]

In Rome, Chausson was shocked by still another modern feature, the tourist: "It is true, this unfortunate country is overrun by Englishmen, Germans, etc., briefly, by all the most thoroughly stupid travelers from all the so-called civilized countries; you have to resign yourself to that in advance; you have to expect to hear newly-weds talk of nothing but furniture in the Sistine Chapel and to see old Englishwomen threaten the holiest virgins of Botticelli with their long teeth."[9]

Yet, all things considered, Italy helped Chausson regain his balance completely. His last letter from there is filled with reflective and mature judgments: "I am very glad to have seen this country again after a long interval of time, I see it better now and I find in it at the same time the charm of a vision of my youth. The same holds true of Italian painting as of the Greek and Latin classics which we are taught not to understand in our *lycées*. Later we return to them and love them, because we find in them something different from what we had been shown."[10]

The quiet ease and serenity of Italy held its spell only for a short while. Upon Chausson's return to Paris, he was faced with the task of completing the music for Maurice Bouchor's drama *La Légende de Sainte-Cécile,* which had its *première* on January 25, 1892. Apparently his late return from Italy had

[8] Wednesday night, 1891.
[9] Rome, November 16, 1891; to Poujaud.
[10] Rome, November 16, 1891; to Poujaud.

Ernest Chausson

left Chausson little time to rehearse the performers, for it was
generally agreed that this first performance was extremely
poor. Any hope he might have had of gaining favor with the
music critics was quickly dispelled by the reaction of the
press—a storm of protest against his music broke loose, sharp-
er than any he had experienced heretofore:

> A musical party sets itself the task of adding harmonies to
> verses, but its celestial voices, to tell the truth, are more cruel than
> the tortures of Gaymas (M. Martel, in *La Justice*).
> The music of M. Chausson is ugly, shrill, thin, grating, badly
> written for voices and instruments. . . . (Ballaigue, in *Revue des
> Deux Mondes*).
> . . . Little anemic numbers, without inspiration, crammed full
> of curious dissonances, but puerile and useless in their continuous
> playful searchings for effect: those starved for sickly dissonances
> were served to perfection (*Le Guide Musical*).

The most interesting negative criticism came from the
critic of *La Vie Parisienne:*

> I reproach M. Bouchor for one more thing: that of having
> entrusted the music for Sainte-Cécile, the patron saint of music,
> to M. Chausson. It seems that, grammatically, his music is good.
> But what would you say of a poet who were to employ nothing
> but the imperfect subjunctive all the time; that might perhaps be
> correct, but it certainly would be exasperating and disagreeable
> to listen to. Such is the music of M. Chausson.

That is indeed how Chausson's composition must have
sounded to an ear accustomed to hearing the melodies of
Gounod, Massenet, Thomas, and Offenbach. It would be

unjust to accuse all these dissenting critics of bad faith. To be sure, some of them did not even listen to the works they condemned; others, literarily rather than musically trained and used to music which appeals on first hearing, were sincere in their judgments. Unfortunately, the ones who had the necessary musical training were attached to one school or another, so that their criticisms were heavily flavored with prejudice.

Yet, not all music critics were hostile to the Franck school. Among those who rallied to its defense was Henri Gauthier-Villars, writing under the pen name of "Willy." Today he is perhaps best known for having been the first husband of the celebrated writer Colette, but in the late nineteenth century his music criticisms enjoyed great popularity in Paris society. In his columns, filled with rapier thrusts and elegant invectives, Willy would often devote as much space to those present at the concert as to the music, especially if he did not like the latter. This apparent flippancy notwithstanding, Willy lent his enthusiastic support to new works in which he saw merit, and Chausson eventually became one of his favorite composers.

Of equally great help to the Franckists was the friendship of the famous violinist Eugène Ysaÿe. Like the *bon vivant* Willy, this big, jovial Belgian presented a rather striking contrast to the more reserved and serious Chausson; if anything, this difference in disposition only served to deepen their mutual affection. Chausson had dedicated his Concert for piano, violin, and string quartet to the Belgian virtuoso in the hope of having him perform it, and Ysaÿe did not disappoint his friend.

Ernest Chausson

It was decided to have the Concert *premièred* in Brussels. There the *Salon des XX* (managed by Octave Maus, who became one of Chausson's most devoted admirers) provided the friendly atmosphere indispensable for the success of a new work. As Chausson was on the Riviera, Vincent d'Indy took charge of the necessary arrangements. Rehearsals had begun, and all seemed to be going smoothly when suddenly the pianist selected to play the solo parts of the Concert returned the score, complaining that the work was too difficult. D'Indy was in despair and wrote to Maus: "The affair of the pianist . . . is most annoying. Chausson counts absolutely on the performance, it will be the ultimate disillusion for him, he will leave for Algeria and never return. It would be a disaster if Chausson is not played that night and it would grieve me deeply."[11]

Fortunately, Pierre de Bréville discovered the young pianist Auguste Pierret in Paris, and so the Concert was performed as scheduled on March 4, 1892, with Pierret and Ysaÿe as soloists, assisted by the Crickboom Quartet. Here, for the first time in his life, Chausson could hear one of his major works played by an outstanding group of artists. The performance was a complete success. Chausson was thrilled. What a difference there had been between the reaction to his music in Brussels and Paris! There his symphony had been rejected by conductors as too difficult; here, in Brussels, not only the Symphony but *Viviane* and his music for the *Tempest* as well had been greeted with enthusiasm. And now Chausson's Concert, a most unusual work, was receiving praise without a dissenting voice: "I feel sure that this week

[11] Madeleine Maus, *Trente années de lutte pour l'Art* (1884–1914), 138.

spent with you will give me spirit and self-confidence. I scarcely know myself since my return from Brussels; I have never been so light-hearted and happy and I cannot think of you all without emotion. I feel that I am going to do far better work than before, and it is to you that I shall owe this."[12]

Chausson finds that it is now his turn to counsel his younger friends who are plagued with the same uncertainty which had troubled him. In answer to a letter from Raymond Bonheur he writes:

You say you blush at the selfish security of your existence. Do not blush but use the time which this security gives you to work for others, for those who need help and support; forget yourself and give of yourself: we must return to the maxim of the Gospels.

. . . I am convinced that there are in Paris hundreds of men with the same preoccupations and desires who do not know how to change their aspirations into action. In our age, aspirations are no longer sufficient. Action is needed. . . . A work of art too is an action, perhaps the most significant which a man can accomplish. I don't know whether we should believe, as Edgar Poe says, in the eternal reality of thoughts, of all thoughts—this thought makes me shudder—but I believe firmly in the reality of expressed thoughts, and a thought can only be considered expressed when it is dressed in a sufficiently beautiful form. To be convinced of that and to continue, as I do, to write music, is that not a ridiculous ambition, the pride of a fool? I hope not. If I do not accomplish what I would like to do—which is only too certain—I shall always achieve what it is in my power to do. Beyond that I need not to worry. The angels have said: Peace on earth to men of good will. If I ever should succeed in producing the work I would like to

[12] Vincent d'Indy, "Ernest Chausson," *Cobbett's Cyclopedic Survey of Chamber Music*, I, 266.

write, it would not be a drama or a symphony but a simple folder of very intimate piano pieces which one would never want to play except in solitude.[13]

It was in this state of mind that Chausson completed the song cycle *Poème de l'Amour et de la Mer,* which he had begun some ten years previously. Octave Maus interested a Belgian singer, Désiré Demest, in the composition, and the latter added a few inquiries about Bouchor's poem to Maus' letter. Chausson's reply is doubly interesting, for it not only shows his love of Belgium but also some of the problems which a song composer faces:

Dear friend:

I can't get over it: What? a singer who is interested in the meaning of what he is singing? One has to go to Belgium to find one of that caliber. And not one word about his voice! about the lack of effects, etc. That is unheard of! And besides, a tenor! Well, I am extremely happy to have come upon him. Surely, it is for Belgium that my music is written.

I have just looked Bouchor's verses over again. Yes, it is true, they are hermetic. But what can be done about it? The idea of printing the words is excellent and the only remedy I can see. . . . And, if you judge it proper, each song could be given a sub-title. I don't insist on it, it is all the same to me, but it is true that one must at least understand the general meaning which bears a Carrière-like imprint. In that case, here is what I would suggest, but if you can find something better, use it without consulting me:

I. *La Fleur des Eaux*
Pressentiment—Rencontre—l'Adieu

[13] November 14, 1892; to Bonheur.

His Life: 1889-93

II. *La Mort de l'Amour*
En mer—l'Oubli—Epilogue

I am leaving out the *Interlude* which I would be too much afraid to play.[14]

Thus the Chaussons traveled once more to Belgium, where on February 21, 1893, Désiré Demest, accompanied by Chausson at the piano, sang the first performance of the *Poème de l'Amour et de la Mer*. Madeleine Maus fondly recalls the appearance of Ernest and Mme Chausson: "I can see this harmonious couple again: she, delicate, slim, with light-golden hair, and eyes of childish blue; he, with eyes of a deeper blue, 'iris eyes without a smile,' beard and brown hair, aquiline nose, a magnificently constructed head and that serious face, brightened at every moment by an affectionate and jovial smile."[15]

Matters were quite different when, later in the year, the *Poème de l'Amour et de la Mer* was performed in Paris in its original version, i.e. with orchestral accompaniment. Chausson knew he was no longer in Brussels when he picked up the *Figaro* the next morning and read the following criticism:

M. Chausson was badly inspired the day he wrote the *Poème de l'Amour et de la Mer;* we admit, however, that the inspiration has some relation to the music which this member of the Société Nationale writes. It moves in crushingly monotonous developments; not a theme can be seized, not a single new harmonic

14 Madeleine Maus, *Trente années de lutte pour l'Art,* 153.
15 *Ibid.,* 153.

series, not a single orchestral detail to make one stop and listen; nothing but a vague and unstressed declamation, nothing but a continuous use of procedures and formulae of what was but recently called "the new school," procedures and formulae which are already outmoded and which have become more unbearable commonplaces than those for which we reproached our grandfathers. Such is this *Poème de l'Amour et de la Mer,* of interminable length and of deadly boredom.

The critics had changed their tune. Now the Franckists were no longer too modern but already out-of-date. Perhaps the critic of the *Figaro* left before the performance was over, for his article does not even mention the last song, which Chausson had modestly entitled *Epilogue.* It is none other than the famous *Le Temps des Lilas,* today the most-frequently performed of all his songs.

1893

THE preceding years had been filled with such feverish activity that, in the spring of 1893, Chausson decided to take time out for a rest. His in-laws had rented a large home in Luzancy (Seine-et-Marne department), where the entire family joined them. As Debussy happened to be near by in Paris, Chausson invited his friend to spend some time with them: "We are still counting on seeing you next Monday. And I am looking forward in advance to the nice days we shall spend together. . . . And perhaps the new Moussorgsky scores will be here. Borrow all the Russian music you can find.

"Bring along something to do. Lerolle is going to paint in the country and I am going to finish my battle scene [of *Le Roi Arthus*]. We'll each work in his corner which, how-ever, will not prevent us from being together at the evening parties."[1]

Debussy and Chausson had been friends for some time. In 1891, Debussy had dedicated *La Mer est plus belle* (Ver-laine) from his *Trois mélodies* to Chausson, and this invita-tion provided an opportunity for them to renew and to deepen their friendship.

[1] Chausson to Debussy; 1893.

Ernest Chausson

The two musicians differed in almost every respect: Debussy was unsettled, financially insecure, and temperamental; Chausson was surrounded by a happy family, was wealthy, generally even tempered, and mature. Yet, in spite of these divergences of character and situation, the two needed each other. Debussy needed someone older and more mature than he, in whose friendship and judgment he could feel secure and from whom he would not mind an occasional chiding; Chausson, on the other hand, needed the stimulus of a younger man like Debussy, especially at a time when, after having given his best measure, he was stubbornly taking up work on *Arthus* again.

Those must have been delightful days, days filled with music and never ending discussions. Since Debussy had become interested in Russian music—especially Moussorgsky—Chausson had sent for the score of *Boris Godunov,* which Debussy played on the piano while Chausson turned the pages for him. The camera has immortalized this scene in which the composers are surrounded by interested listeners of all ages—not the least of these was Henry Lerolle, a faithful friend of both men. Another photograph shows them with Raymond Bonheur, who had first introduced Debussy to Chausson. No doubt, many other artists dropped in from time to time, turning the calm country-retreat at Luzancy into a nineteenth-century Ferney.

Although the two musicians soon had to separate, the time they had spent together in Luzancy had cemented their friendship so strongly that a steady flow of letters kept them in close touch with one another. Debussy was the first to express his feelings: "It is so good to have each other's confidence in all kinds of subjects, for even in friendship one often feels taken aback by certain painful thoughts and that is like people who have a beautiful garden and surround it with iron-lanced fences. So, long live those who throw their doors wide open to us. You may answer me that there are gardens whose flowers do not let themselves be picked, but we shall never end the discussion and I prefer to tell you that your intervention in my life is surely one of the experiences dearest to me and I think still more of it than I can say."[2]

Chausson's reply leaves no doubt about the deep impression which Debussy has left:

Dear friend:

How I regret that you are no longer here! That is, however, the only thing I can reproach you for. I had become so much accustomed to seeing you!

Now the gates of the château remain open in vain, everything has changed. No more Russian music, no more boat-rides, no more billiard games. . . .

We have had an interlude of real childish frivolity; that is over. What is not over, fortunately, is the intimacy which has been established between us. The affection which you show me is very precious to me and I am deeply touched by it. I am so sure of it that you are certainly one of those with whom I engage most gladly in conversation, because I feel that with you I have nothing to fear by showing myself as I am, even in my bad features. And that is one of the greatest charms, and one of the rarest, of friendship. You know you can count on mine, absolutely.[3]

Shortly thereafter, Chausson left for the South of France;

[2] May 7, 1893.
[3] Luzancy, Sunday, 3 o'clock, 1893.

as for Debussy, he was heartbroken by the absence of his friend: "Ah, my dear friend! What a Sunday! A joyless Sunday it was without you. Had you been here the atmosphere would have been a delight to breathe, for I must tell you that if I already loved you very much, the few days spent in your company have made me for always your devoted friend. But I will not try to express my emotion here. However lyrical I might become, I should not do myself justice.

"Yet this is not so laughable as you think. It was so good to feel that I belonged somehow to your family and that I was part of you all. But am I not going too far, and won't you feel my friendship to be rather a nuisance? I wish so much to please you that sometimes I imagine things that decidedly are crazy."[4]

Even while the two friends were apart, they kept each other constantly informed on how their work was progressing. Interestingly enough, both of them were engaged in the composition of an opera, Debussy on *Pelléas et Mélisande* and Chausson on *Le Roi Arthus,* which he apparently abandoned temporarily for the setting of Maeterlinck's early poems, *Serres chaudes:* "And now you are hostile to the Serres chaudes and, even though you punish your generous heart to suffer by being inclosed in a blue mood and to inhale flowers which are brittle from too much sunshine, do not fail to bring me what you have written. I am very anxious to see that, for it is hardly necessary to assure you of my complete sympathy for your music and of my conviction that, if you will only continue to listen to yourself alone without paying attention to the chorus of those affected but annoying frogs, you will

[4] June 4, 1893; quoted in Edward Lockspeiser, *Debussy,* 67.

produce great works. Let me tell you something, since the occasion presents itself and since I may perhaps not dare do so in another way: you are very much superior to those who surround you and you are so by virtue of your sensitiveness and artistic tact which, in my opinion, seem to be completely absent in the others. . . .

"I am terribly pained by your absence and feel like a little side path that has been abandoned in favor of the highways; sometimes I permit myself the melancholy illusion of going as far as to your door and upon my return I am accompanied by the sad thought that your door will not be open for a long time. Do not think ill of this sensitiveness and, above all, do not believe it to be affected."[5]

In August, Chausson returned briefly to his Paris home, where Debussy visited him almost daily. Chausson's departure, this time for Royan, left Debussy once more disconsolate: "You down there and I here with nothing to do. . . . It hurts me to have caused you sadness because of my bad luck, you, one of the rare men who fully merit happiness, for you show with such affectionate grace those aspects of it which are usually carefully hidden. And, as everything in you is so grateful, I am deeply happy to love you with all my heart, since in you the man completes the artist. And, whenever you are willing to show me some of your music, you cannot imagine with what ardent friendship I listen to your expression of feelings which I have been denied, but which, expressed by you, fill me with joy; and, if at times I have spoken to you a bit harshly about it, blame only the impatient side of my character. . . .

[5] Debussy to Chausson; Paris, May 22, 1893.

Ernest Chausson

"As for your sermons, they are always very dear to me; you are somewhat like a big, older brother in whom one has complete confidence and from whom one even accepts an occasional scolding; and forgive me if until now I have not succeeded in satisfying you, but rest assured nevertheless that any reproach from you would grieve me so much that it is impossible for me not to do all in my power so as never to deserve any."[6]

Shortly after Debussy's birthday, he addressed this reflective letter to Chausson:

And now the hour of my thirty-first year has struck, and I am still not very sure of my aesthetics, and there are things which I still do not know (how to write masterpieces, for example, and being very serious among other things, having the defect of dreaming away my life too much, and of seeing its realities only at the moment when they are becoming insurmountable). Perhaps I am more to be pitied than blamed; at any rate, in writing this I am counting on your pardon and your patience. . . .

Truly, music should have been a hermetic science, protected by texts so difficult to decipher that it would certainly have discouraged the flock of people who use it with the flippancy with which one uses a pocket handkerchief! Now, beyond that, instead of propagating art among the public, I propose the foundation of a "Society of Musical Esotericism". . . .

LATEST NEWS

C. A. Debussy is completing a scene from *Pelléas et Mélisande*, "A fountain in the park" (Act IV, scene IV), on which he would like to have the opinion of E. Chausson.[7]

[6] August 26, 1893.
[7] September 6, 1893.

His Life: 1893

Chausson, sensing the uneasiness of the younger man and no doubt recalling his own struggles, hastened to reply:

Dear friend,

Well, at last a good, long letter from you, proving that you are no longer ill, which makes me glad. The scene of *Pelléas et Mélisande* finished! And the fourth *Prose lyrique!* How you go at it! I would like very much to hear all that. I know in advance that I shall like it. I cannot say as much of *Le Roi Arthus*. He is causing me much distress, and repeatedly so. For, when I think I have finished a scene, I notice, after a few months of rest, that there are many things in the words that do not fit. I change them and, naturally, I have to change the music too. It always has to be done over again and will it ever end? That it must, however. I have lived long enough with adultery and remorse; I am strongly tempted to express other, less dramatic feelings.

To be "very sure of one's aesthetics," good heavens, that is quite a job. You complain that you are not settled at the age of thirty-one. What am I to say, being no longer thirty-one and torn by uncertainty, gropings in the dark and uneasiness?

It seems to me quite on the contrary that you know quite well what you want to achieve. But my impression is perhaps not the same as yours; and you are the only good judge in that matter. Finding yourself, throwing off your shell, getting rid of many opinions adopted sometimes without quite knowing why (because they seduced you one day or because they were presented to you by people you like and admire) and which nonetheless do not entirely correspond to your intimate nature, that is the problem and it is terribly difficult.

Allures of a "young barbarian" . . . to be truthful, I think you have more "young barbarism" in your hair than in your mind, and your music reflects essentially modern and refined feelings. And the foundation of a "Society of Musical Esotericism" is not very typical of the VIth century, either. But since we have repudiated the old romantic taste for local color! . . . And how justly; about this subject there would be many things to say, so many in fact that I give it up.[8]

Not all the Chausson-Debussy letters were complimentary, though. The two musicians were outspoken in their criticisms, as only those can afford to be who have no doubt about the motivation which lies behind a critical remark of the other. Thus Debussy: "One thing I would like to see you lose is your preoccupation with *undertones;* I believe we have been led into that by the same old R. Wagner, and that we think too often about the frame before having the picture, and sometimes the richness of the latter makes us pass over the poverty of the idea; I am not speaking of the case where magnificent undertones dress up ideas comparable to dolls worth thirteen sous! We would gain, it seems to me, by taking the opposite attitude, that is to say, finding the perfect design of an idea and surrounding it with just the most necessary ornaments, for truly certain people are like priests who place incomparable gems on wooden idols! Look at the poverty of symbols hidden in several of Mallarmé's last sonnets, in which nonetheless the skill of an artistic craftsman has been carried to the limit, and then compare this with Bach, where everything contributes fully to bring out the idea, where the lightness of the undertones never obscures the principal idea. . . ."[9]

[8] Royan, September 7 (?), 1893.

[9] Undated letter, addressed to Chausson, Villa Clara, Arcachon. Probably written in October, 1893, because it mentions Debussy's efforts in arranging

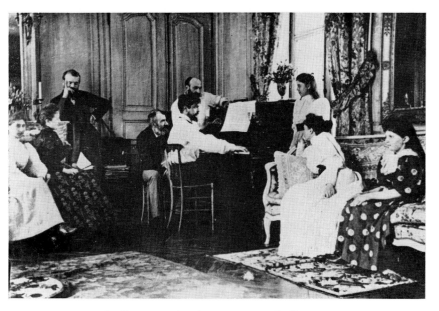

At Luzancy in the summer of 1893

Persons identified (*left to right*): Mme Henry Lerolle (*seated, in black dress*); Raymond Bonheur (*chin in hand*); Henry Lerolle; Ernest Chausson (*turning pages*); Claude Debussy (*at piano*); Mme Chausson (*seated on couch, in white dress*).

His Life: 1893

Chausson's reply shows that, far from taking offense at these remarks from his younger friend, he appreciated Debussy's keen power of observation: "As for myself, I have taken up again, and without too much trouble, my third act. I am not dissatisfied with what I am writing at the moment. It seems to me that it is becoming clear and de-wagnerized. My wife for whom I played the first scene told me that she almost did not recognize me. But I suppose that is a bit exaggerated. Otherwise, can you imagine me in a position of having to do the first two acts all over again! That would be equivalent to abandoning the drama, because I feel incapable of going over all that again. It is time to finish it and to go on to something else. You are a thousand times right in what you say about my preoccupation with 'undertones'.

"While you were writing me I thought just about the same thing, the beginning of my third act proves that. I believe I owe that preoccupation especially to the Société Nationale. Its concerts resemble oftentimes a kind of doctoral examination. You have to prove that you know your craft. That is a great error; doubtless, knowing one's craft is necessary, but it is still more indispensable to have one's individual craft. A work of art is not a thesis and in it skill should never be anything but a secondary quality. All that does not deny that the Société Nationale has rendered great services and is still the place in Paris where we hear the best modern music."[10]

Chausson was apparently as outspoken in his judgments

a cover design for the Concert, a project to which he refers in a letter dated October 2, 1893.

[10] Undated letter, probably written in October or November, 1893.

Ernest Chausson

as Debussy. The latter had sent him his Quartet for appraisal, and seemingly Chausson offered a number of objections, for Debussy writes: "I began the Wagnerian performances last Saturday; it went very well, nobody flinched, not even Mme A., who did not even talk! As for me, I was worn out and that Wagner is decidedly a tiresome man.

"Now, need I say that all that does not replace you and that I find the exile from your friendship very long; I am so fond of you. Need I also say that for a few days I was very much grieved by what you said about my quartet, for I felt that I had only made you like *certain things* more, whereas I had hoped that it would make you forget them. Well, I shall write another one, just for you, and I shall try to clothe it in more dignified forms. I would like to have enough influence on you to be able to scold you and to tell you that you are fooling yourself! You exert so much pressure on your ideas that they no longer dare appear before you for fear of not being dressed up properly. You do not let yourself go enough and, above all, you do not give free reins to that mysterious thing which makes us find the impression of a feeling that is just right, when persistent and obstinate research is bound only to weaken it. I am so thoroughly convinced that you have within you all the desirable expression that I am pained when I see you enervate yourself in useless struggles; we must realize that we are nothing in the face of art, we are merely the instruments of destiny, but must we also let it take its course! Perhaps I don't have the right to speak to you this way, but forgive me and see in it only a great desire to see you what you should be and that as much as possible, because you are more capable of it than anybody;

so take of this only what you want, you will easily realize that I have no intentions of giving you advice!! but I would simply like to give you courage to believe in yourself."[11]

It would be difficult to measure the effect of this close relationship on Debussy and Chausson. The letters of the former, written in an emotional style, leave little doubt about the deep impression which Chausson had made on him. Regarding Debussy's musical production during 1893 and 1894, it is worth keeping in mind that he consulted his friend while composing parts of *Pelléas et Mélisande* and the *Proses lyriques*,[12] and that Debussy wrote his Quartet with the intention of submitting it to Chausson's judgment. We could even speculate that, had Chausson's reaction been more favorable, Debussy might very well have dedicated it to him.[13]

As for Chausson, there is every indication that he was profoundly stirred by his close association with Debussy; in fact, it can be said that, artistically speaking and with due respect for proportions, the effect of Debussy on Chausson resembled that of Rimbaud on Verlaine. In both cases the older man had already produced a few important works and

[11] Undated letter, probably written in February, 1894. There is a reference in it to a "Festival Debussy" to be held in Brussels on March 1; see Lerolle's letter on p. 37n.

[12] One of these, *De fleurs,* is dedicated to Mme Chausson.

[13] Léon Vallas, *Claude Debussy,* 63, makes this comment on their musical relationship: "Chausson's harmonic tendencies and those of Debussy were closely related although the tastes and training of the two men were so divergent, and they certainly reacted to one another. A comparison of the works of the two friends about 1884 [*sic;* obviously, 1894 is meant] reveals traces of their reciprocal influences, though they are difficult to determine definitely." Vallas also finds that the principal melody of Debussy's *Rondel* from *Trois chansons de France* (1904) recalls Chausson's *Chanson perpétuelle.*

was beginning to become somewhat settled, when the younger one burst into his life with disturbing consequences. As Verlaine had done, Chausson had been experimenting with new forms and expressions (perhaps less strikingly so, but the Concert was nevertheless a daring experiment), when his intimate friendship with Debussy made him realize that the younger man was engaged in musical researches which were, in effect, far more revolutionary and far-reaching than anything Chausson had ever dreamed of. Finally, Debussy's taunts (for that they were, however politely and respectfully Debussy expressed them) did not fail to attain their mark any less than those which Rimbaud had addressed to Verlaine, with a resulting fear in the older man that he, who had thought of himself as belonging to a young and radical movement, was turning stale and sterile, while a new musical tendency was opening up new paths. Consequently, the self-confidence which Chausson had gained after the Brussels performances of his works soon gave way to new soul-searchings. These reappraisals, coupled with a determined effort to complete *Le Roi Arthus,* brought on a new crisis in his life.

1894

IN 1894 eight years had passed since Chausson first had
sketched the outlines of *Le Roi Arthus,* and the end was
not yet in sight. To be sure, the composer had repeatedly
abandoned his opera in favor of other, more tempting, projects: the Symphony, the Concert, the *Poème de l'Amour et
de la Mer, La Légende de Sainte-Cécile,* and, just recently,
the *Serres chaudes;* but the opera weighed on his mind, and
eventually he would return to it as if driven by a guilty conscience. This usually necessitated a revision of what he had
previously written in order to bring it into harmony with the
new ideas he had acquired during the interval. Although he
did not compose swiftly, no other work of his required a
comparable amount of time. On the surface this may seem
surprising, for Chausson's excellent background in literature
and his interest in dramatic music seemed to qualify him
eminently to handle the opera. As the work progressed, however, two major difficulties became more and more apparent:
Chausson wanted to express his fundamental ideas in this
work[1] and therefore strove for greatest perfection; the second

[1] We shall endeavor to deal in more detail with this matter in Chapter
VII, Part Two.

obstacle could not possibly be avoided by anyone attempting to write a lyrical drama at that time—the struggle with Wagner.

Thus, when Chausson returned to *Arthus* late in 1893 with the firm determination (almost with clenched teeth, it seems) of completing the work without further interruption, he was inevitably heading for a crisis similar to the one he had experienced during the composing of the Symphony. Then he had faced the test which was to decide whether he could successfully write a large-scale work; now the problem was far more difficult: to write an opera based on a legendary subject without succumbing completely to Wagner, a task somewhat like writing a fugue that is not to be reminiscent of Bach.

An examination of Chausson's references to Wagner in his letters indicates that his early admiration for the German master had been subject to considerable modifications in the course of time. Upon submitting the first draft of his opera to Poujaud, Chausson had added: "The greatest defect of my drama is without doubt the analogy of the subject with that of Tristan. That would still not matter, if I could only successfully de-wagnerize myself. Wagnerian in subject and Wagnerian in music, is that not too much altogether?"[2]

Subsequent remarks, such as "the red specter of Wagner" or "that frightful Wagner who is blocking all my paths," show Chausson's constant effort to struggle loose from the tyrannical hold which the giant from Bayreuth exerted over the lyrical drama. Not that Chausson ever denied Wagner's accomplishments, but he had gradually come to realize that

[2] Cannes, 1886; to Poujaud.

uncritical admiration of Wagner would amount to surrender-
ing his own personality. By 1893, Chausson had become
frankly critical of the German composer: "Some two weeks
ago I prolonged a visit with my father in order to hear the
Walküre at the Opéra. Oh! without any profound happiness.
That interpretation, that performance, that atmosphere, it is
not the same any more! And the work itself has changed with
time. I was deeply sorry for having come to see it. How
strange that now *we* are finding some passages in Wagner
less juicy than others! And I surprise myself thinking about
the 'romance du printemps,' about things which I formerly
would have covered with blasphemy."[3]

Chausson's letters during this crisis appear less violent
than those of 1889–90, but they reveal an inner struggle no
less intense, even if less externalized, than the one he had
endured during the creation of the Symphony: "I am like an
ant that encounters a big, slippery stone in its way. A thousand detours are necessary before a passage can be found. . . .

"I would like to find something really good, and I don't
even find something really mediocre. I do a little revising in
the afternoons. That is to say, I clean up things already done.
It is very complicated and difficult."[4]

It would be unreasonable to attach undue importance to
these occasional outbursts of despair, even of rage, in Chausson, for they can readily be explained by the particular difficulties he was encountering at the time, and they constitute,
on the whole, a far from ordinary element in his letters; quite
on the contrary, the testimony of those who knew him inti-

[3] Luzancy, June 12, 1893; to Poujaud.
[4] 1894; to Bonheur.

mately pictures him as a gentle, considerate, and kind person. It is true, however, that a considerable portion of his music conveys an uneasy sadness. "The most profound and agitated melancholy is, indeed, expressed in almost his entire music: discreet and almost unobtrusive in *Paysage* (Corot could not paint a more gently sad gray), more present in *Soir de fête,* in the andante of the Unfinished Quartet, sharp and poignant in the third movement of the Concert, in the *Chanson perpétuelle;* profoundly tragic in the *Poème,* it attains almost sublime proportions in the 'très calme' of the Piano Quartet."[5] To which another critic adds this important qualification: "The prevailing mood of Chausson's music is an entrancing melancholy, tender and twilit, a melancholy free from whine or maudlin sentiment; . . . it is . . . expressed in terms of the utmost sensitive refinement, subtle beauty and aristocratic distinction of manner."[6]

It is equally true that the poems which Chausson selected for his songs express, almost without exception, a similar mood. He chose his texts from a wide variety of poets—romantics, Parnassians, and symbolists—and, excepting men like Bouchor and Mauclair who were his personal friends, his sound knowledge of literature usually guided him to the works of France's great poets, such as Gautier, Verlaine, Villiers de l'Isle-Adam, and especially Leconte de Lisle. In his choice of poems Chausson displayed a decided preference for those which expressed elegiac sentiments. Time and again, in *Nanny,* the *Poème de l'Amour et de la Mer,* the

[5] M-D Calvocoressi, *"A la Mémoire d'Ernest Chausson," l'Art Moderne,* Vol. XXIII, (May 24, 1903), 137–39.

[6] Kaikhosru Shapurji Sorabji, "A Note on Ernest Chausson," *Mi Contra Fa,* 119.

His Life: 1894

Serres chaudes, the *Chansons de Shakespeare,* and the *Chanson perpétuelle,* love plaints alternate with despair and resignation.

As might be expected, the critics have been struck by the disparity between this aspect of Chausson's music and the exterior circumstances of his life. It has puzzled them that a man who was healthy, happily married, surrounded by an affectionate family, and free from financial worries should have written music that is saturated with a recurring melancholy. In the absence of evidence, they have engaged in more or less wild speculations. The influence of Schopenhauer's philosophy on Chausson, his intense awareness that he was more fortunate than many others, his constant quest for musical expression that would be equal to his ideas, or perhaps even a mysterious event in his life which may have cast a tragic shadow over his happiness—all these have been suggested as possible explanations.

As we have no new evidence to offer, we shall refrain from adding to these speculations; it must be pointed out, however, that, tempting as it may be, the effort to establish a parallel between a composer's music and his life is frequently contradicted by the facts. For example, *"Siegfried* rouses one's admiration the more when one thinks that it was the offspring of sickness and suffering. The time at which Wagner wrote it was one of the saddest in his life. It often happens so in art. One goes astray in trying to interpret an artist's life by his work, for it is exceptional to find one a counterpart of the other. It is more likely that an artist's work will express the opposite of his life—the things he did not experience."[7]

[7] Romain Rolland, *Essays on Music,* 324.

Ernest Chausson

Chausson had occasionally commented on his melancholy moods. In a letter of 1876 he had attributed them to his relative solitude caused by associating mainly with people older than he; eight years later he discussed the subject from another point of view, that of a happily married man:

> My reading, especially Balzac and Stendhal, had stuffed me with ideas, not false for everybody but false for me; in the situation in which I have the good fortune of being, *"La Physiologie du Mariage"* and *"l'Amour"* appear to me as no more than books full of wit and finesse but very dangerous. In a clearly-defined situation the straightest, the least cautious and the least clever way of life is actually the cleverest and the safest. The prudence of which Balzac speaks often borders on defiance. As for the subtle feelings which Stendhal exposes, simple and true love which, I believe, is the only lasting one in marriage, hardly ever worries about them.[8]

Finally, while reporting his interminable difficulties with *Arthus,* Chausson exclaimed: "Good heavens, I know very well that I am what people call fortunate, almost frightfully so. And, doubtless, I would be too much so without this wretched, uneasy and violent brain of mine."[9]

The critics have seized on this "enigma" in Chausson apparently because it hinted at some possible excitement in his otherwise unsensational life, and they have been tempted to emphasize this aspect at the expense of others which are at least equally important. It is noteworthy in this respect that no less an authority than Pierre de Bréville, a colleague and close friend of Chausson's, interprets his music quite differ-

[8] Paris, November 19, 1884; to Mme de Rayssac.
[9] 1894; to Bonheur.

ently: "It may be said that all his works exhale a dreamy sensitiveness that is peculiar to him. His music is constantly saying the word *'cher.'* His music is not passion in disorder: it is always affectionate, and this affection is gently agitated in its discreet reserve. It is, indeed, he himself that is disclosed in it—a somewhat timid man who shunned noisy expansiveness and delighted in intimate relationships. . . . He has been charged with melancholy, but he was not a sad man. The melancholy that veiled his soul veiled also from his eyes the vulgarity of exterior spectacles. He had no reason to fear or to avoid vulgarity, for he knew not what it was."[10]

To be sure, Chausson was subject to somber reflections—he was even occasionally haunted by a premonition of premature death. But he was not at all the ponderous, melancholy, neurotic, and lonely man which some critics make of him. His frequent association and correspondence with his colleagues, his many friendships, the receptions at his home, and the affection of his family kept him from slipping into loneliness; his letters reveal him as a man of wit and humor, and, although he can hardly be called a businessman, he had nonetheless to take care of the real estate he owned, and Chausson's frequent absences from Paris did not exactly facilitate these matters. On one such occasion he had to appeal for aid to his mother-in-law:

I have just received a tearful letter from one of my tenants. . . . He tells me that, having been ill, he had his mistress come over to take care of him, that since that time the concierge has been so much wounded in her virtue that she has made life miserable for him by going so far as to pursue him through the halls with an

[10] *Mercure de France,* September, 1899.

ice pick (in Athalie's times they called it a dagger), insulting him coarsely and wanting to throw him down the staircases, or rather the staircase, for there is only one. He concludes by saying that he is sending a complaint to the police and by asking me to fire the concierge. All that is very unusual. I have answered him that I regretted all these dramas, but that, being absent from Paris, it was impossible for me to make an immediate decision and that I would commission someone to look into the matter and to do what he would consider necessary.[11]

Chausson's smiling and subtle humor, which this letter shows again, is perhaps too frequently overlooked. It is also present in his music, even if possibly less pronounced than his lyrical qualities. For examples of the humorous facet in his personality, we need only turn to the "intermezzo" of his Trio or to the last movement of the Concert.

One cannot speak of Chausson's character without mentioning his unselfishness. In the execution of his duties as secretary of the Société Nationale de Musique, he usually showed far more concern about the works of others than about his own. His friend Octave Maus accused him one day of neglecting his personal interests, asking him: "But, after all, what are you doing at the moment? Do you have a project, are you working on something?" "Yes," said Chausson, "I have accepted the task of making up a catalogue of everything that has been performed at the Société Nationale since its founding; this list is needed and I hope to do better than just a secretary. I am busy at present collecting the programs."[12]

[11] Undated letter.

[12] Camille Mauclair, *"Souvenirs sur Ernest Chausson,"* *La Vogue,* August 15, 1899.

His Life: 1894

From Chausson's letters and from the souvenirs of his friends, we can piece together the picture of a man with a rich personality and with wide interests; we are, therefore, inclined to discount as misleading Mauclair's claim that "he did not like people, his amiability hid his graveness, his gaiety was often a deference towards others."[13] It is true, however, that only few people knew him intimately, for, due to his *"pudeur,"* he very rarely expressed himself freely in letters or even in conversations with his closest friends. It took a severe crisis, such as he was suffering in 1894, to make him confide in someone. We do not know who this friend was[14] nor what Chausson told him, but the letter which he wrote him afterwards leaves no doubt that such a conversation did take place. This letter, although mentioning no details, permits perhaps the deepest insight into Chausson's inner life:

You must have been unable to understand anything I said to you the day before yesterday. As I never tell everything, I would surely be much better off if I never told anything. But one is not immune from certain moments of weakness and I saw you in one of those moments. The atmosphere of Paris, which I believed would do me much good, produced the opposite effect. I am at present calmer here. It is not yet a true, deep calmness, but I become necessarily less unreasonable. . . . Don't imagine anything unusual . . . but it is impossible for me to talk about it, even to you. Why? I do not know; several times I was about to do so and yet some internal impulse made me say words completely contrary to what I would have wanted to say. So, since after all it is not at all necessary to speak about it, I have not tried to do so any more.

13 *Ibid.*

14 It was most likely Henry Lerolle or possibly Vincent d'Indy, two of the few people Chausson addressed familiarly in his letters.

Don't mention this letter to me when I shall be seeing you in a few days. A conversation such as would certainly ensue would be bad for me at this time. ... I would not have written you today if I had not been a bit ashamed of the weakness I displayed the other day and perhaps also if I had not just spent a whole day in solitude, which calms better than any words.[15]

A comparison of this letter with the one written during the height of the 1889 crisis[16] will show how much Chausson had matured during the intervening years. This time there were no desperate cries, no curses—just a momentary weakness followed by a strong recovery.

[15] Liège, 1894.
[16] See Chapter IV.

1895-96

INSPIRATION is a capricious thing; it cannot be forced to come to the surface by sheer determination. Chausson had learned this lesson from bitter experience, so that, in spite of his resolution to complete *Le Roi Arthus,* he heeded a call to come to Brussels where two of his works were scheduled for performance. For several years now Paris had continued to turn a deaf ear to his music; in fact, the last important performances of his works in that city had taken place in 1892: the fiasco of his *La Légende de Sainte-Cécile* and a repeat performance of the Symphony at the Société Nationale. Since then not even the latter work had found favor with the most important French conductors—Lamoureux had ignored it while Colonne considered it too difficult for his orchestra. In 1895, Brussels honored both of these works with a performance: that of *Sainte-Cécile* especially proved a complete delight for the composer, for it was done by first-rate artists: Georgette Leblanc[1] and the Ysaÿe Quartet.

". . . a performance once in a while is necessary for composers with little faith in themselves," Chausson had written

[1] The reader will recall Miss Leblanc as the famous heroine of Maeterlinck's symbolist plays.

to Poujaud in 1886, and now, thanks to his friends in Brussels, he could return to his work with renewed confidence. However, before settling down to his final struggle with *Le Roi Arthus,* the composer permitted himself the fulfillment of an old wish. He had always wanted to write intimate piano pieces yet had not done so since the *Cinq fantaisies* (1879), an unsuccessful composition and subsequently destroyed. The calmness of *Paysage* for piano expresses more eloquently than words the composer's victory over the anguish which had obsessed him during 1894.

It was only fitting that for the completion of *Arthus,* his favorite work, Chausson chose his favorite place—San Domenico di Fiesole:

We see all Florence, the hills, the olive trees and above it all a marvellous sky with sunsets and incomparable moons. How beautiful this country is! And how I love it! I do not tire of it. You cannot imagine how much good it does me. Since being here, I find myself completely changed, light, happy; I have rediscovered the beauty of beautiful joy. It seems as if I am returning home after a long and unpleasant trip and finding myself at ease again. For it cannot be denied, I was becoming bitter. This interminable *Arthus* had turned sour with time and had just about poisoned me. After a few violent fights I have finally gained the upper hand and now I am burying him very gaily under a heap of orchestral pages (the rough draft of the second act alone takes up 235 pages)! ... Now that the composition is finished and that I have decided to modify a few details only, I am gradually able to look at my drama more calmly and, if I cannot judge it as yet, I can at least realize a little what it is like. You know that I do not sin from an excess of self-confidence; I shall perhaps surprise you by saying that this time I am not dissatisfied. I hope that this drama will be a bit human

Chausson and his wife
on their honeymoon trip, Basel, 1883

and not too much in the fashionable style. At least, that is what I wanted to accomplish. But will it seem that way on the stage? Here my doubt begins again. Since only a performance can enlighten me on that subject, I am going to get busy upon my return to see where there is a chance of finding a place for this "Roi."[2]

On Christmas Day, 1895, after nearly ten years of toil, Chausson signed the last page of *Le Roi Arthus*. At last his mind was free; henceforth, he could devote his undivided attention to new works, conceived with constantly growing maturity and perfection.

Although Chausson had not dared interrupt his work on the opera, new ideas, new projects had impressed themselves on him during his stay in Italy. He concludes the letter just cited by writing: "My sojourn here will not have any direct musical influence. However, there are many things which I am tempted to write—pure music this time—and which have been inspired in me by the landscapes or works of art here. I had such a low opinion of my musical talents that I was surprised when I saw what ideas certain paintings awaken in me. Some of them give me the entire outline of a symphonic piece. I shall have to try writing one when I am free again."

Was it one of these inspirations which produced the exquisite *Poème* for violin and orchestra? If so, the composer, anxious perhaps to defend his "pure music" against the interference of program notes, guarded his secret well. In fact, there is an air of mystery surrounding the whole composition. It is not mentioned in his letters, which leads us to assume that it was finished in a relatively short time and without the

[2] San Domenico di Fiesole, Villa Rondinelli, 1895; to Poujaud.

usual difficulties; the seamless solidity of the work seems to lend further strength to this view. The *Poème* was probably written between April and August, 1896, for the *Serres chaudes* had been completed in March, *Quelques danses* for piano in July, two of the *Trois lieder* in September, and October finds Chausson in Spain.

This trip to the other side of the Pyrenees was occasioned by a series of concerts in Barcelona which were dedicated to French music. At one of these, on October 31, at the Teatro Lírico, Chausson conducted his Symphony. Although the Spanish critics were divided in their reactions, they all agreed that the performance was greeted by strong applause. As for the composer, he was baffled by the behavior of Spanish audiences: "What an amazing public! Nothing but applause or whistling. At least they have got life in them. We did not have a large crowd. It was raining. Now, here that is a disaster. At the end of the second concert, as it was raining, some people remained in the lobby of the Lirico until six o'clock in the morning (!!). Just imagine what would happen if we, in Paris or Brussels, refused to leave when it is raining!"[3]

During his stay in Spain, Chausson renewed numerous friendships and made many new ones. Perhaps the most memorable event of this trip was an excursion to the home of the Catalan painter Santiago Rusinol. The party included, among others, Chausson, Ysaÿe, their wives, Guillet, Morera, and Granados. As happens when musicians get together, they played music for twelve hours, and it was at this artistic gathering, in October, 1896, that Eugène Ysaÿe performed the as yet unpublished *Poème* for the first time.

[3] Paris, Saturday morning, 1897; to Vincent d'Indy.

His Life: 1895-96

It is not certain whether or not Isaac Albéniz was present at this party, but he probably heard the *Poème* at some time during Chausson's stay in Spain. When Albéniz had been in Paris, bewildered, unhappy, and without friends, Chausson had opened his home to him and his family, an act of generosity which the Spanish composer repaid in a royal manner. Touring Germany in the spring of 1897, Albéniz first approached Arthur Nikisch, the conductor of the Berlin Philharmonic Orchestra, and induced him to include the Franck group in his forthcoming Paris concerts. Next, Albéniz, with the score of the *Poème* tucked under his arm, presented himself at the publishing house of Breitkopf & Haertel in Leipzig. But there he met with less success. Breitkopf, judging the music "too modern to please and sell," flatly refused to publish it. But, of course, if Albéniz were willing to pay for the cost of publication ——. Determined to get the work printed, Albéniz agreed to Breitkopf's terms; and, in order to prevent any possible suspicions on the part of Chausson, the Spanish musician added another three hundred marks as royalty for his friend. When this was arranged, he informed Chausson by postal card of his accomplishments.

The unsuspecting Frenchman was thunderstruck and replied at once: "You are a darling—what powerful strokes! In but a few days you manage to arrange matters for us in the most miraculous way. Nevertheless, it was not that easy. The arrangement with Nikisch fills me with joy: I have to laugh at the mere thought that perhaps one of my works will be played in Paris by a German while the French conductors want to have nothing to do with me unless Ysaÿe is involved. . . . And the three hundred marks! Why, do you know that

that is quite a fortune? What merry-making we shall have!
. . . Thank you, admirable friend, incomparable courier of
musical works, paradoxical friend! How can it be possible
that you take so much interest in us? I am tempted to wonder
whether you are really a colleague of ours."[4]

Albéniz' carefully laid plans nearly came to naught when,
in June, Chausson, on his way to Prague, stopped over in
Leipzig. Informed of this ahead of time, Albéniz hastily sent
instructions to the publisher. Thus, upon his arrival, Chausson was greeted by Breitkopf in person, who treated him with
exceptional courtesy, praised the *Poème,* which was about to
appear in print and, when taking leave, tactfully handed him
the three hundred marks which Albéniz had deposited for
that purpose. The deceived composer, who had never received any such treatment from a publisher, had to seek for
words to express his gratitude for Breitkopf's kind reception
and generosity! Still unable to believe what has happened, he
writes to his wife: "I just come from Breitkopf's, everything
went very well and smoothly. This may sound silly, but I
must confess that I took great pleasure in collecting those
three hundred marks."[5]

The *Poème* received its first public performance at a concert of the Conservatory Orchestra in Nancy, in December,
1896. Again Ysaÿe was the soloist, and Chausson, who was
present, made a brief speech in honor of the great violinist.

Encouraged by the initial success of the composition,
Chausson attempted to have it performed in Paris. Thanks

[4] March, 1897; to Albéniz. Quoted in Michel Raux Deledicque, *Albéniz,
su vida inquieta y ardorosa,* 263.

[5] June, 1897; quoted in *Ibid.,* 227.

to the provision that Ysaÿe was to be the soloist, the *Poème* finally had its Paris *première* on April 4, 1897, at the Concerts Colonne. Chausson was listening backstage in the Châtelet Theater; with him was Camille Mauclair. Suddenly, Chausson heard a loud burst of applause coming from the theater, and his friend saw the most sincere look of stupefaction coming over his face. "As we went down together on a winding staircase, he put his hand on my shoulder and, with his delicate smile: 'Don't say anything about it,' he whispered, 'I don't want to seem ... but I can't get over it.' "[6]

This was the first time Chausson had heard applause from a Paris audience other than that of the Société Nationale. More important still, a few hostile critics joined in, to wit Joncières who reported in *La Liberté*: "Now, I must confess that today I took real pleasure in listening to the very interesting piece for violin by M. Chausson. The idea is certainly not banal but charming in its gracefulness and simplicity. Its full, striking harmonies follow logically without ever hurting the ear." But there were the usual dissenting voices, even though a bit more cautious than on previous occasions. Torchet of *l'Evénement* was disturbed: ". . . despite the swooning of the young and old aesthetes, I persist in thinking that it is music such as should not be written, useless, even harmful music, because, in spite of the composer's talent, it contains not an idea and fills us with great boredom." G. Salvayre, in *Gil Blas,* moreover, did not pull any punches: "As for the so-called poem by M. Ernest Chausson, it is one of the most tedious samples of the great 'school of stew without

[6] Quoted by G. Carraud, "Ernest Chausson," *Le Menestrel,* Vol. LXXXII (April 2, 1920), 137–39.

meat' that I have heard. It is pretentiously sterile and empty. I deplore sincerely that an artist of M. Ysaÿe's stature, who has so many beautiful things to play for us, should besmirch himself with such unwholesome music (if that can still be called music) which, as the name of its author indicates, must have been manufactured in prison."[7]

Time has proved Albéniz and Ysaÿe right and M. Salvayre wrong, for the *Poème* has become a great favorite in the violin repertory. Yet today it matters little that a publisher refused the work and that a critic heaped abuse on it; what should not be forgotten, though, is the story of a singularly unselfish friendship which deserves to be evoked whenever the work is played. Chausson never learned of the Spaniard's generosity,[8] yet we cannot but consider a man happy who had the good fortune of counting Albéniz among his friends.

[7] a poor pun: in French, *chausson* can mean a slipper as well as a pastry.

[8] It was revealed in a letter, dated May 22, 1931, from Albéniz' daughter to Mme Chausson.

1897-99

IN spite of Chausson's detractors, interest in his works began to grow. The Symphony was performed four times in 1897: in Brussels, Bordeaux, Paris, and even in Russia (where Chausson's name was not entirely unknown, his *Viviane* having been performed in St. Petersburg as early as 1892). Of these, the Paris performance of the Symphony was by far the most memorable. It must have given Chausson great satisfaction that, at the urging of Albéniz, the German conductor Arthur Nikisch had decided to undertake a task which the French conductors had scorned so far, yet it is ironical that the first major performance of the Symphony in France was given by the Berlin Philharmonic Orchestra during a guest tour, on May 13, 1897, at the Cirque d'Hiver.

The unveiling of this work to the general public was not an unqualified success, but Chausson's friends felt that he had taken an important step forward, now that one of Europe's great conductors had placed the Symphony on his program. Their eagerness to read the next day's reviews was ill-rewarded; the work was hardly mentioned and, as usual, the opposition was led by Torchet of *l'Evénement*: "If M. Nikisch wished to satisfy the young musicians . . . he should not have chosen M. Chausson—a difficult author, the Mallarmé of music—as a representative, but M. Gustave Charpentier, this composer of free genius. . ."

The friends of the author were indignant or distressed, according to their temperament. Chausson himself lost in no way his gentle smile: "Come now, forget those wretched things," he said repeatedly, "if my symphony is good, the critics will come to appreciate it sooner or later."[1]

Hearing his Symphony played by an outstanding orchestra must have given Chausson the self-confidence he needed, at least so it would seem, for henceforth he gives the impression of being a changed person: complaints about his work become very rare, giving way to the kind of calmness for which he had so desperately hoped during the anguished year of 1894. To be sure, now and then he alludes to a snag in his efforts: ". . . I am working on a piano quartet and on an orchestral piece. When it goes well I am happy and when it does not, I grit my teeth just so I won't lose the habit."[2] But even the tenor of these remarks reveals a marked difference from the black moments of bitterness which had spotted his letters in previous years. Much more typical of his state of mind is a reminiscing note, addressed to Vincent d'Indy:

The other day, as I was reading through old letters, I found a bundle of letters from you. That brings to my mind that it will soon be twenty years (one should not say that) that we have known each other, and during all that time we have not once found an occasion to quarrel or to belittle each other, or to play

[1] Henri Gauthier-Villars (Willy), article of June 19, 1899, *Garçon, l'Audition!*
[2] (Summer), 1897; to Poujaud.

each other one of those skillful nasty tricks which are the greatest refinement of certain artists—at least they are called such—; not the slightest chicanery; not the least prick of jealousy. You know, that is not at all ordinary.[3]

Along with this increased stability, Chausson displays renewed vigor and activity. Anxious to put *Le Roi Arthus* to the test, he made every effort to have his opera performed. Attempts to get it staged in Spain, Belgium, and Germany had brought no results, but, in the spring of 1897, Neumann, a director in Prague, was showing an interest in the work. Would Prague once more appreciate a composer who was scorned at home? For a while it almost seemed so. Encouraged, Chausson hastened to Prague, where he was happy to meet Albéniz again; the latter was negotiating a performance of his *Pepita Jiménez,* and the two friends exchanged ideas on their respective projects. Albéniz reports to his wife: "Chausson is delighted and does not stop urging me to abandon any modernistic trend and to devote myself to writing what I feel, inasmuch as I feel it so strongly; the man cannot get over his enthusiasm and his praise has made me immeasurably proud."[4]

While engaged in the somewhat tedious preliminary talks with the director, Chausson addressed a very tender letter to his wife. It almost seems as if, as in the letter to D'Indy, he is paying a last tribute to those dearest to him:

What a nuisance the theater is! Once and for all, I want no

[3] Paris, Friday morning, 1897.
[4] Michel Raux Deledicque, *Albéniz, su vida inquieta y ardorosa,* 273.

more of it. If I have to spend the coming winter at it, my whole summer's work will be lost. Wouldn't it be wiser if I sent it all to the devil and left only posthumous works? Not that I do not easily realize that I am exceptionally fortunate. But never mind morality and philosophy. I'll admit anything at all, but I desire terribly to see and to embrace you; everything else seems infinitely less important to me. You do not know that I was obliged to admit that I am an absolutely faithful husband. Albéniz wanted to prove to Schalk that there is not a single married man who does not have a few brief adventures which entail no consequences and which would not affect marital fidelity in any way. As he tried to line me up as a witness with repeated "isn't that so's," I had to say that such was not my case. Whence exclamations! "It is true," Albéniz replied, "that your wife is so beautiful, so intelligent, so kind . . ."[5]

A few days later the negotiations were successfully concluded. Chausson sends this note to his mother-in-law: "He [the director] is taking it, as you already know from the telegram I just sent you a little while ago. . . . On first impulse I was too astonished to be happy (which does not make a bad impression on the director); now I am slowly getting used to it and am happier about it."[6]

His joy was premature. Choudens, the publisher of the opera, hoping for a *première* in Paris or Brussels, refused his consent. For once Chausson is angered and discouraged. Informing Octave Maus of his latest failure, he concludes: "Let us leave the field to Bruneau and Wagner. Not without regret, for it seems to me that I am better at writing dramatic

[5] Prague, June, 1897.
[6] Prague, June 25, 1897.

92

music than symphonies. But what can be done about it? Time passes; the years drift by; our illusions fall.[7]

These successive disappointments might have driven Chausson to the verge of despair only a few years ago, but since 1896 he had gathered enough strength and confidence to continue releasing the creative power which he had stored up during his final work on *Arthus*. In rapid succession he produced two major compositions at just about that time: the *Pièce* for cello and piano (Opus 39) and the Piano Quartet in A Major.

[The Piano Quartet] was to mark a culminating point of his work; and here it is evident that he had made an immense stride forward, quite as much in the merit and charm of the ideas as in the novelty of the form, in which cyclic constituents, rhythmically modified, end by acquiring a double nature, which enriches and greatly strengthens the architecture of the work.

It is a curious thing, especially when one reflects that the quartet was written only two years before the composer's death, that, in this work, sadness seems to have given place to confidence. In fact, although the second cyclic theme (which appears first in the opening of the slow movement and reappears in the finale) is always in the major key—yet retaining an undoubted melancholic character—one might say that Chausson, free at last from his doubt and his distress, thinks only of a flight to new and loftier regions of art, into which a way—hitherto unexplored—will open for him, a way so soon afterwards debarred to him by an unforeseen catastrophe.[8]

[7] (Probably July or August), 1897.

[8] Vincent d'Indy, "Ernest Chausson," *Cobbett's Cyclopedic Survey of Chamber Music*, I, 267.

Ernest Chausson

The Piano Quartet was composed at Veyrier (Haute Savoie), near the Lac d'Annecy. This work not only elicited very few complaints in letters but was also terminated in record speed, at least for Chausson: the first movement is dated September 17 and the finale October 23, 1897. While in Veyrier, half-amazed and half-amused, Chausson informs his wife that he has received 391 francs in royalties, a sure sign that his works had been receiving increasing attention of late.

The *première* of the Piano Quartet took place on April 2, 1898, at a concert of the Société Nationale with Auguste Pierret, to whom it is dedicated, playing the piano. Of all the works *premièred* during Chausson's lifetime this was by far the best received, with most of the applause going to the second and third movements.

On April 18, 1898, the Symphony in B flat Major was again performed at the Société Nationale, this time almost against Chausson's wishes. He had planned a program which was to include Albéniz' *Catalonia* and *Ouverture de Shéhérazade* by Maurice Ravel—then a struggling composer of twenty-two—but D'Indy, now president of the Société, vetoed these selections: "You always forget yourself in favor of others," he wrote to Chausson, "but this time I want your Symphony to be performed." D'Indy recalled, no doubt, that the date of the concert marked the seventh anniversary of its *première*.

Along with the Piano Quartet, Chausson had been working on an orchestral piece to which he gave the title *Soir de fête*. This represented actually his third excursion into the field of the tone poem, the first two being *Viviane* and the

destroyed *Solitude dans les Bois.* The occurrence of tone
poems in the Franck school, which took pride in devoting
itself to "pure music," may seem somewhat surprising;
Chausson himself had repeatedly expressed his dislike for
descriptive music yet had admitted his inability to write like
Bach and Haydn.

He [Chausson] owed to César Franck not only the maxims
which governed his artistic life but also his particular concept of
music. He wrote a few significant pages of filial piety about that
glorious composer. Some critics had reproached Franck for not
possessing all the skills of his profession; he answered them: "It
is loftiness of ideas and depth of feeling that make great musicians." And further on: "He does not use sounds in order to
describe material things or to express literary ideas. For him music
is a language sufficient in itself, which has particular and mysterious laws." He was obliged to admit that, undoubtedly, Franck
himself was unfaithful to his doctrine and that a symphonic poem
such as *Le Chasseur maudit* is very much like descriptive and literary music; he, moreover, preferred the divine *Béatitudes* and the
ingenious Quintet and, in the Quintet, he placed the andante
above all the rest, because in it he recognized the shadings of his
own sensitiveness. . . . The two sentiments which the disciple inherited from the teacher were exactly this contempt of technical
skill and the passion for pure music. By this two-fold trait, he is
among all the musicians of his time closest to César Franck and
furthest from M. Camille Saint-Saëns. He felt that music must
move us by its intimate virtues, without telling any story, without
describing anything, and he thought that it possesses this power
due to the sensitiveness of the artist and not due to his skill.[9]

[9] André Hallays, *"Le Roi Arthus," Revue de Paris,* Vol. VI (December
15, 1903), 849. While it is true that Chausson placed the sensitiveness of a
musician above his skill, he considered sound musicianship an indispensable

Ernest Chausson

Chausson's musical judgments bear witness to his detestation of works in which he thought the composer had resorted to using lush effects to gloss over the lack of genuine emotions. After listening to a performance of *Cavalleria Rusticana,* he wrote: "There is much shouting in it, which perhaps gives the public an illusion of intense feelings. As for the orchestra, it makes one think of an agricultural fair in a sub-prefecture. If I were a trumpet player, I wouldn't like to play that! the poor man does not stop for a minute and all the time fff. . . . Truly, there is nothing like shortcomings to make us see clearly."[10] And, regarding Rimski-Korsakov: "Try as I may, I cannot share your admiration for *Antar*. It is not my fault. I have played it several times with a great desire of liking it; I can't. I find it old stuff; a mixture of romanticism and orientalism; rather little music and, except at the end, no emotion. I have begun looking through the orchestral score. It amazes me very much."[11]

It seems inconsistent that the author of these judgments is also the composer of such "impure" music as *Viviane, Solitude dans les Bois,* and *Soir de fête.* The explanation is simply that Chausson lived at a time when literature domi-

---

tool of a composer, as witnessed by the following letter to Gustave Sama-zeuilh: ". . . I prefer to see you courageously at grips with a string quartet, which is defending itself. That is, indeed, their traditional way, they almost always defend themselves! And with them one is never certain of having the last word. . . . But let that not interfere with working hard on perfecting your technical skill. I frequently hear the assertion that modern artists know their craft marvelously, but that they don't have any ideas. That is silly and completely false. It is because a great number among them do not know their craft well enough that the ideas *which they do have* do not come forth with enough force and clarity."

[10] Quoted by Charles Oulmont, *Musique de l'Amour*, 90.
[11] Crémault, September 3, 1889; to Poujaud.

nated the arts. Verlaine and the symbolist poets had broken down the barriers separating word and sound, and at Mallarmé's home poets and musicians established as close a union as had ever existed between the two arts in France; it is no accident that the French art song reached its apogee in the late nineteenth century. We have already had several occasions to note the role of Wagner in France; the fusion of the arts, which he proposed, did not fail to leave a deep impression on French music. No composer, no matter how independent, could completely escape the pressure of these convergent influences. Franck and his entire school produced numerous tone poems and even Fauré, the purest non-Wagnerian, bowed to the literary demands of his time with such works as *Shylock* or the *Pelléas et Mélisande Suite*. As for Chausson, he was far too well read, far too fond of painting to write music that would not, in some measure, reflect the emotions which these works had instilled in him. His compositions contain elements of such suggestiveness that one critic was moved to write:

He had exquisite feeling, and was one of the first to understand in what degree literature and the graphic arts could influence present-day music.[12]

His music is full of murmurs of the swaying of branches, of fresh flowers suddenly scattered on his stealthy passage—full of freshness and of life, of nature and of calls uttered through foliage whose shady density opens at times in the path of a warm ray. It is at once ingenious and skilful music, and resembles the fairies, the water-fays, the elves, and Merlin the magician, expert in philtres and in the gathering of simples.[13]

[12] G. Jean-Aubry, *French Music of Today*, 94.
[13] *Ibid.*, 132.

Ernest Chausson

Even Chausson's "pure" works have drawn similar comments. Thus Maurice Bouchor compares the andante of the Symphony to a prayer, "penetrated with a sentiment of the irreparable but devoid of desolation. It does not call for revolt, either: it accepts the destiny of man, which is to live in drama."[14] And the *Poème* for violin and orchestra suggested a most romantic story to Antony Tudor for his ballet *Jardin aux Lilas* ("Lilac Garden"), a story of which, we suspect, the composer would have heartily disapproved.

What differentiates Chausson from his contemporaries is that, while many of them continued pursuing the marriage of music and the other arts until consummation (for what else is musical impressionism?), his tone poems show a development which tended to turn away more and more from narrowly programmatic music. He conceived of the tone poem not as a slavish translation of literary themes, but rather as the orchestral extension of the song, in which the title merely serves as an inspiration to indicate the mood but in which no story is told, no text interpreted. While *Viviane* had been accompanied by rather detailed program notes, *Solitude dans les Bois,* so far as we were able to gather, contained but few literary indications.

Soir de fête, Chausson's last tone poem, was presented with hardly any explanations at all. Its *première,* on March 10, 1898, was generally well received, except for a few condemning criticisms. The applause of the audience seems to have been no more than lukewarm, though. A few months later Vincent d'Indy conducted the work in Barcelona during a concert of French music and sent this note to Octave

[14] *La Revue Musicale* (December 1, 1925), 188.

98

His Life: 1897–99

Maus: "Battle over Chausson's *'Soir de fête';* in spite of obstinate defenders, the whistles won over the applause."

On October 23, 1898, *Soir de fête* was performed again, this time in Brussels. Maus sent some of the criticisms to Chausson, whose reply sheds much light on his attitude towards the tone poem:

Dear friend:

Thank you for the newspaper clippings. It is always amusing to see how what one has thought is received in the listener's mind. Judging from what I have read in the Belgian papers, I do not seem to have made myself very clear. That is not especially astonishing, for nothing is more difficult. I never intended to depict a real celebration, popular or otherwise; I know very well that that would have been more easily understandable, but I have not done it, because I am almost sure that I would have done it very badly. And, moreover, that is not at all what I am trying to express musically. I simply wanted to note down a personal impression of the distant noise of a crowd; as contrast, the calm and serene night. The difficulty lay in the transposition. To give the idea of a joyous throng without employing any of those rhythms and phrases which seem obligatory in characterizing a celebration. For a moment I thought of it. I even considered interjecting and mixing them in. Upon returning from the parade, the *Marseillaise* and the Russian hymn. Evidently that would have been infinitely clearer. However, I gave it up. It seemed to me that that would debase my subject considerably. My celebration was limited to France, almost to the environment of Paris, while the one I was thinking of was nameless, without family and without country. . . . But I realize that if one has the preconceived idea of a realistic "fair," *"Soir de fête"* must appear to be a kind of wager on an obscure and incomprehensible subject.[15]

[15] Quoted in *Revue Belge de Musicologie,* Vol. III, No. 2 (1949), 116–17.

Ernest Chausson

As in the case of *Viviane,* Chausson intended to revise the score of his latest work and therefore did not have it published during his lifetime. After his death, his family felt that publication of *Soir de fête* would have been against his wishes, so that the composition has remained unpublished.[16]

During the remainder of 1898, Chausson returned to writing songs which included the *Deux poèmes* (Opus 34) to texts of Verlaine, *Cantique à l'Épouse* and *Dans la Forêt du Charme et de l'Enchantement* (Opus 36), and the moving *Chanson perpétuelle* which Camille Mauclair considered "the most beautiful lied with orchestra . . . in French music"[17] and which Louis Laloy describes as "so serious, so noble and so tender with an orchestral accompaniment in which everything sighs and sings like human voices."[18]

The year 1899 opened with great promise. Never before had Chausson mapped such ambitious plans: he was writing a string quartet, sketching the opening of a second symphony, and preparing the libretto for a new opera, *La Vie est un Songe* ("Life is a Dream"), based on a play by the seventeenth-century Spanish dramatist Calderón; in addition, he was planning to write a sonata for violin and piano. This is no longer the timid, uncertain musician who had writhed for two years to compose a symphony, who had cursed his songs in a moment of despair, who had slaved for ten years to produce an opera—here is a master aware of his

[16] The original ms. of the work is in the *Bibliothèque Nationale* in Paris; all performances have been played from this ms.

[17] *La Religion de la Musique,* 234.

[18] Quoted in *S.I.M.,* Aug.-Sept., 1910.

capacities and anxious to pour out the full measure of his great gifts.

On January 29, 1899, Chausson traveled to Le Havre in order to hear the first performance of the *Chanson perpétuelle,* sung by Mme Jeanne Raunay, to whom it is dedicated. At the same concert he conducted selections from his incidental music to *La Tempête.*

That same month the name of Chausson covered the greatest distance it encompassed during his life. The occasion was a performance of *Viviane* in Moscow (the third time one of his works was played in Russia) at which an American critic was present who provides us with the following review in *Musical America:*

A novelty of very promising originality was the number three of the programme, a Symphonic Poem by Ernest Chausson. Who is Ernest Chausson? it was asked with no little curiosity. Judging after the design and the workmanship of his composition, Ernest Chausson must belong to the modern French school. . . .

Of course, Chausson has closely studied the modern masters of orchestration, and Wagner in particular, but there are very few motives or even fragments of motives that could be called downright reminiscences. The composer is not only striving for originality; no, he possesses originality in no small degree, and [*sic*] this symphonic poem his opus 5, we are to expect much greater things from him yet. Like most of the young composers of the day, he scores masterfully.

That was some six months before Chausson's death. For the time being, however, there seemed to be not a cloud in the sky. It even began to look as if *Le Roi Arthus* would at last find its way to a stage; in fact, there were two good possibilities. In Karlsruhe, Germany, Felix Mottl had been highly impressed by the work and was getting ready to perform it in 1900. This hope, however, was also to come to naught, because the Grand Duke of Baden, Mottl's employer, had made other engagements. On his way home, Chausson made his usual stop in Brussels, where he read the score to MM. Kufferath and Guidé who promised to perform it if they ever obtained the directorship of the Théâtre de la Monnaie, a promise faithfully kept—even if too late for the composer.

While in Belgium, Chausson looked up Georgette Leblanc, who had sung the lead in *La Légende de Sainte-Cécile* in 1895.

It is a pity that you are not here. I am sure that you would be very much impressed with Georgette. She is an admirable and versatile artist. I would very much like to have her sing Guinevere [in *Arthus*]. That is even absolutely what I would need. I have shown her a little of the music. She likes the first act well, the death delights her. The second act has ruffled her a bit, but that is hardly surprising with my interpretation of it, and for the first time at that. I believe, on the contrary, that it is just made for her.[19]

With the arrival of the first hot days, Chausson left Paris for his country home at Limay, near Mantes. He still could not work at his best in the capital and there was yet much to be done: the string quartet was "defending itself," the beginning of the second symphony was sketched, and he hoped to write at least the first movement. It was also necessary to start

[19] March 30, 1899, to Lerolle.

thinking of the music for his new opera; he had just completed the libretto in which he had adapted Calderón's somewhat unwieldy play to operatic proportions by discarding several minor characters and centralizing the plot. As in *Arthus,* Chausson had impressed his own warmth on the libretto: the half-savage hero is humanized by his growing love for a woman who makes him see the gentler side of life. Life is a dream! What a perfect theme for the composer of whom Camille Mauclair had said: ". . . he always seemed to get up and, in the midst of a dream, take a step forward towards real life."[20]

Early in June, Chausson had completed the first two movements of the string quartet, but the third, a scherzo, was putting up a vigorous fight. The composer had learned from experience that not much is accomplished by flying into fits of despair. At least here, in the country, he could take long walks or else go bicycle-riding for a while. The fresh air and the soothing countryside would soon impose their calmness on his troubled mind. After all, time was in his favor; he was still young, at least for a composer: only forty-four. *"Le Père Franck"* might have lived to be a hundred if it had not been for the unfortunate accident which cost him his life—and how much wonderful music he could yet have written.

There were other gaps in the ranks of the Franck school: Lekeu had died at the age of twenty-four, Castillon at thirty-five, and Henri Duparc had been forced to give up composing because of illness. But there were good signs too. D'Indy had taken over as head of the Franckists and, besides Chausson, Pierre de Bréville, Charles Bordes, and Guy Ropartz

[20] *La Vogue,* August 15, 1899.

were helping him perpetuate the work of their teacher. The future of the school seemed assured, for young musicians were eager to study with them; one of these, Gustave Samazeuilh, had been consulting Chausson frequently and had just sent him a letter asking for advice on his first work. Times had changed indeed! How often had he written letters like that himself—to Chabrier, to Duparc. It was best to answer at once; perhaps it would be a consolation to Samazeuilh that he too (the young man addressed him as *"maître"*) was encountering obstacles in his own work.

... I am not surprised that your first work is giving you trouble. I have not reached my goal, either. A few days ago I thought that my Scherzo was going to be finished very soon and now I find myself stopped by an unexpected difficulty which I cannot overcome. At least for the time being, for I hope, nevertheless, that I shall succeed in having the last word. . . . Do not be discouraged and keep on working. . . . Now, here I am on the fourth page. I have to get back to that confounded Scherzo! Perhaps I am going to find the missing link after this intermission.[21]

This undated letter was probably written on June 9 or 10; it was perhaps the last letter he wrote.

On June 10, 1899, Chausson went bicycle-riding along a sloping road which he used to take almost every day. At the bottom of the slope he lost control of the bicycle and smashed into a wall. He was killed instantly and with him many justified hopes for great works to come.

Chausson's sudden death left his family and friends stunned. They were unable to comprehend this stroke of fate,

[21] Quoted by G. Samazeuilh, *Euterpe* (July, 1949), 118.

come upon them without warning like lightning on a clear summer day. At the funeral they came together once more, his friends, to say a last farewell to the man who had had no personal enemies and whose tragic loss made them realize how much he had meant to them. The procession included the composers Duparc, Fauré, Benoît, Dukas, de Bréville, Louis de Serres, Debussy, Albéric Magnard, Alfred Bruneau, Charles Koechlin, Sylvio Lazzari, André Messager, Albéniz, and Samazeuilh; the painters Degas, Carrière, Besnard, Redon; the sculptors Rodin, Charpentier, Lenoir; the writers and performers Henri de Régnier, Pierre Louÿs, Pierre Lalo, Henri Gauthier-Villars, Raymond Bonheur, Paul Poujaud, Eugène Ysaÿe, Raoul Pugno, and Octave Maus.

Pierre Louÿs expressed the feelings of Chausson's friends in a letter to Mme Chausson: "There was never a more excellent man than your husband; I knew it and hardly ever proved to him how much I was struck each time by his frank look, his firm handshake, and by the admirable goodness which manifested itself in all his gestures. At every moment of his life he needed to make people happy. Everybody loved him. At least, speaking for myself, I loved him very much, believe me. And I have never told him so; we always think there is time and that we will always see again those who are young."[22]

A performance of the *Poème* was scheduled in London for June 17, 1899, a week after Chausson's death. He had planned to attend this concert; perhaps it was better this way, for he would have been deeply hurt by the London papers which

[22] Quoted by Charles Oulmont, "*Deux amis, Claude Debussy et Ernest Chausson,*" *Mercure de France,* Vol. CCLVI (1934), 248–69.

Ernest Chausson

referred to him as a "gifted amateur." After the performance, Ysaÿe addressed the following letter to Chausson's children:

Today, June 17, 1899, three thousand listeners, informed of the composer's death, listened pensively and religiously and with an emotion that I felt to be increasing—to his *Poème* in whose sad and sublimely plaintive melody I let my heart sob. Your father has received today—I affirm it, for I felt it very strongly—the first leaf of a crown of glory, which all the peoples will weave for him; and I, who was among the first to understand, love, and admire the intimate musician, the sincere and gently melancholic poet he was—I was today still more moved at the thought that I was the first after his death to place humbly all my artistic strength at the service of one of his works, whose pure beauty will reflect itself on all of you.

Many similarly touching letters of consolation were sent to the bereaved family of the composer. But it was the usually so clownish Henri Gauthier-Villars who paid the most moving tribute to the composer of *Le Roi Arthus:*

The musician whom we sadly escorted on Thursday was certainly less known by the general public than any hack writer of lucrative operettas. It is no surprise that he enjoyed but very little public renown—he had never written anything but good music: let us recall the lofty inspiration, the proud character of his symphony, his Concert, written luxuriously, with pages of feverish transport; his two admirable quartets; the *Poème* with which Ysaÿe scored triumphs; *Soir de fête,* a musical impression whose poignant contrasts of gaiety and melancholy obtained such a lively success at the Concerts Colonne; a great number of songs, most of them bearing the imprint of that elegiac gracefulness which made his personality recognizable among all others, finally a great drama, *Artus* [*sic*], for which he had himself drawn the poem from the legend of the Round Table, with a skill to which all those who have heard it render homage, writers and musicians alike, Pierre Louÿs as Vincent d'Indy.

It would seem that such a rich flowering of works—I still am far from having cited all of them—imposed upon the critics the duty to call them to public attention. But did they? The critics, as usual, were occupied with less artistic but more remunerative matters. . . .

Ernest Chausson disappears at the moment when he had just acquired the only quality he was still lacking: self-confidence. This perpetual uneasiness, which had tormented him for such a long time with hesitations, had finally been banished by artistic approval after each new performance: incidental music for the *Tempest* and *La Légende de Sainte-Cécile,* the *Poème de l'Amour et de la Mer, Viviane,* and especially the two quartets, which must be counted among the most significant productions of this young school, represented by Vincent d'Indy, Guy Ropartz, Paul Dukas, Pierre de Bréville, Charles Bordes, Louis de Serres, Albéric Magnard, all different but animated by a common faith in Art, inherited from César Franck, and which guides them to the highest summits, unmindful of immediate success and passing acclaim.

He was completing a string quartet whose andante was already asserting itself with a commanding beauty; Madame Jeanne Raunay was going to acquaint the public with the *Chanson perpétuelle,* a marvel of penetrating emotion; Felix Mottl was preparing *Artus* for rehearsals in Carlsruhe and, from day to day, . . . the evolution of this generous mind was pointing towards clearer harmonies, towards more freely singing melodies, towards Joy!

Towards joy, alas! And this vast production, and these still greater hopes, and this infinite affection for his family—for no man ever loved nor was loved more—all that is shattered by an idiotic accident: a bicycle runs down a slope too rapidly and this head, full of noble thoughts, crashes into a wall . . . a corpse is lifted up.

But I say this with fervent certainty—into which my grieving affection for the dear deceased does not enter—Ernest Chausson is one of those who survive their death: "Horrible death never takes them completely!" Now that he is no longer among us to cast aside praises with that artistic modesty, veiled by unmindfulness, which made him hostile to any publicity, his friends, his admirers, and especially the one who, after living solely for him, is now sustained only by the memory of her beloved husband, all of them are going to show the public his worth. And this modest man will enter the gates of glory!"[23]

[23] Henri Gauthier-Villars, in an article of June 19, 1899, in *Garçon, l'Audition!*

PART

2

Ernest Chausson : *His Works*

A Musical Personality

"MELANCHOLY" and *"pudeur"* best designate the dominant traits of Ernest Chausson's personality, let us say French melancholy and aristocratic *"pudeur."* Chausson occupies an almost privileged position between the heavy romanticism of César Franck and the airy impressionism of Claude Debussy. It would be difficult to find in the history of French music a more objectively, a more dispassionately *French* composer, whose personality, in spite of popular credence, ascertained itself successfully against the forceful influences of Wagnerism, Italianism, and Franckism itself.

Chausson's music possesses none of the German's emotional impulses and their attendant moral, religious, and metaphysical implications, nor the often complicated and romantically mystical meanderings of the Belgian. No one will dispute, furthermore, the fact that it is quite removed from the deeply human and descriptive considerations of Italian aesthetics. On the other hand, nothing could be more French than Chausson's constant devotion to the fine nuances of style which carries in itself all the emotional and aesthetic implications he might wish to convey. For this reason, one

Ernest Chausson

could say that his art conceals art; his is truly a style which is imbued with life and significance by means of a subtle manipulation of feelings. To deny the reality or validity of such feelings is to show oneself insensitive to his most essential quality. A performance of his works requires above all, like all great music, a sympathetic creative effort on the part of the interpreter.

Such merit notwithstanding, criticism, both during and after Chausson's short lifetime, has devoted only passing thought to him and felt that the epigram "Wagnerian" sufficed for a general evaluation. To be sure, his stature is not comparable to that of a Bach, Beethoven, Debussy, Verdi, or Wagner; but he is a composer of extreme refinement, exquisite sense of balance, and, as his Piano Quartet in A most conclusively illustrates, convincing depth. If the encroaching idiom of other school-founding composers finds expression in some of his works, it cannot be said that it remained the *"raison d'être"* of these works, nor that it was sought at the expense of his highly talented, though nervous, individuality. No man can escape the pace-setting tendencies of his time. We should even say that if he exerted himself to oppose them, the effort of resistance would have a deleterious effect upon him and warp his output. Dante's appearance was not as miraculous as it would seem in literary histories, nor was Rousseau's completely unheralded. Likewise, Chausson was a product of his age, but rather than accept its general aesthetic values in order to create a new mode of sensitivity by striking out in unexplored directions (we are thinking of Debussy), his reserved nature preferred to accept its values in order to bring their expression to the ultimate in delicacy

His Works: A Personality

and refinement. Along with his contemporaries, he dispensed with much of the traditional classical form but did not bring to the surface the emotional demand which accompanied his thoughts in the manner of a Debussy, a Fauré, a Franck, or even a D'Indy, nor did he share too frequently their desire to be profoundly original. Chausson's inspiration was never dissatisfied with the language of his epoch. Rather than explore, he polished.

Chausson's polishing was a process of weaving the tenuous fabric that exists between straightforward lyrical expression and the restrained sensitization of a hidden feeling. And in this process, which is more tedious and requires more nervous sensitivity than the search for novel effects, he revealed his truly aristocratic temperament, aristocratic in its superior, almost cavalier repugnance of all music that yielded to an effusive emotional abandon and attached itself too literally to plastic significance. This implied a ceaseless effort towards self-contained presentation, and an averred desire to express in music only music itself. Indeed, Chausson's compositions do impress us by what we may call an unwillingness to transcribe *intentionally* the palpitations of the heart or the pulsations of an inspired soul. They exude, instead, a serene wish to seek their own perfection in themselves and to be musical for the sole purpose of being beautiful.

What D'Annunzio so aptly said about Debussy—that he was "a moment in French sensitivity"—might be appropriated for our purposes and applied to Ernest Chausson. Perhaps the term "intelligent sensitivity" would be clearer and more complete. If his premature death had not closed the door so tragically to further creations, he might very feasibly

Ernest Chausson

have become the musical counterpart of his contemporary, the poet Paul Verlaine. By this, we do not contend in any way that the self-possessed, gentle, wealthy, socially prominent, and happily married composer could ever have turned into a *"musicien maudit."* But Chausson was a member of that sensitive and nervous generation of 1880 to 1900 which recognized itself in Verlaine. A *"tristesse saturnienne"* in Chausson's music does remind us unequivocally of the poet of *"Poèmes saturniens," "Fêtes galantes,"* and *"Romances sans paroles."* The same kind of unoppressing nervosity and unburdened fragility exist, which permit us to savor, in melancholy moods common to us all, rare and hidden sensations.

There is turbulence and vagueness in Chausson's scores, and an incompleteness that serves both to obfuscate his deep lyricism and to permit the listener at all times the gratifying intercalation of his personal emotions. And in the mild agitation that accompanies indefinitiveness, there is a continuous upward movement, an aspiration towards an ideal which, by definition, never becoming an achievement, infuses into the composition as a whole a soft feeling of resignation. The idioms of both Verlaine and Chausson are expressed in minor tonalities enriched by dissonances.[1] Their works seem to have a spiritual halo to which their respective idioms cannot do justice and which transcends their meaning, approaching, somewhat insecurely, what Mallarmé called *"l'Azur."* Intelligently contained, their sensitivity embraces willingly the more complicated psyche of melancholy and appears to obey

[1] "Verlaine," *Columbia Dictionary of Modern European Literature,* 850.

Photograph by P. Frois (Biarritz)

Chausson in 1886

certain silent subconscious forces which beckon them to destroy their own happiness.

Chausson's "highly personal" style, as it is usually described, is the result of this conscious sensitivity—French and aristocratic, nervous and controlled. The scrupulous way in which he adhered to it engendered an inner struggle that was like the off-stage secret life of each composition. His natural propensity towards rich lyricism, as witnessed in the *Poème,* clashed with his self-imposed standards of impersonalism, as witnessed in the Trio. The Piano Quartet and many of his *Mélodies* testify that sometimes Chausson emerged the victor in the contest; some parts of the Symphony and the end of the Concert indicate that at other times he could not cope with his own ideal and that he filled certain measures with notes merely in order to satisfy, however imperfectly, the momentum of his idea. For these reasons, his position in the history of music is interesting not only musically, but humanly as well. The critic Oulmont says this of him: "In the perpetual debate between the personal and impersonal, the moral beauty of the man appears, overtaking the individual in order to attain the general. Thanks to this, we leave the too exclusive frame of a personality in order to incarnate the human aspect in a general manner, and we enter the vast realm of the man."[2]

In Chausson, the eternal struggle between reality and aspiration, being and dream, is again symbolized. By way of consequence, his music gains in sincerity and subtlety. Unlike

[2] Oulmont, *"Deux Amis, Claude Debussy et Ernest Chausson,"* Mercure de France, Vol. CCLVI (1934), 116.

Ernest Chausson

Verlaine's poetry in its usual unoriginality in structure and technique, it is, like Verlaine's poetry, unique in feeling, suggestiveness, and refinement. Through it, the composer seems to personify the emotional longings and the mental uneasiness of his generation, which, more than any other, seemed charged with the sadness of a transitory and evanescent world.

Chausson, too, was "a moment in French sensitivity," a moment in the cultural existence of his country.

The Mélodies

CHAUSSON was always aware that he was more at ease while working at smaller genres than at larger ones. Accordingly, his *Mélodies* include some of the most masterfully elegant numbers that the composer has ever scored. More subtle and refined than Henri Duparc, as tenderly melancholic but less movingly somber than Guillaume Lekeu, just as charming but more personal than either Charles Bordes or Guy Ropartz, Chausson establishes himself at the origins of that modern lineage of French song writers—let us say, for greater clarity, of French "lied" writers—which has recently found such worthy exponents in Francis Poulenc and Albert Roussel.

A few words of historical definition are necessary at this point. As Camille Mauclair pointed out,[1] the "lied" differs from the *"chanson"* in that the latter relies chiefly on the text which is emphasized by the melody and rhythm of the music, whereas the former fuses music and text with equal importance in a miniature tone drama aimed at expressing an *"état sentimental."* The one, therefore, is closer to literature; the other, to music. Before the influence of the Austro-German

---

[1] *"Le lied français contemporain," Musica,* November, 1908.

lied in France, the French had only the "romance" which could approach it, however sketchily. For, as the Gounod albums illustrate, the unaltered accompaniment which underlines each stanza, while relying on melody, could not suit the requirements of the "northern" form's varied moods that demanded, often for each verse, a special, polyrhythmic accompaniment, subtly shaded according to the meaning of the words. In this respect, Schumann differed from Schubert; and the disciples of César Franck, preferring a less popular aesthetics of more refined emotions and more elevated thought, took over the German's example and produced a genre which fully merits the designation of French Lied, a genre which is the net aesthetic result of the concomitant influences of Wagnerian ideas, the symbolism of Mallarmé, and the poetic innovations of Verlaine.

To the lied lover, Chausson's *Mélodies* are of very distinct interest, for they represent not merely the most exquisite in his work, but also the most characteristic in French song writing—that is, a kind of concentrated, and thereby intense, intellectualism capable of expressing the most intimate psychological demands through varying rhythms and accents. The styles of Schubert, Schumann, Brahms, and Hugo Wolf have changed, but not the general framework of the lied's artistic meaning.

We might say, however, that the miniature drama effect of Schubert's *"Erlkoenig"* or Wolf's "Prometheus" is not really found, even in the most ambitious of the *Mélodies, La Caravane.* Owing to a number of causes, the German lied, nationally speaking, has translated the innate dramatic propensities of the people and their accompanying capacity for

His Works: The Mélodies

deep feeling, just as Italians in their *"arie"* have striven to reproduce the spontaneous lyricism of their beautiful singing voices. In France, as one critic says,[2] where art is more a matter of fastidious discrimination and good vocal material is not so abundant, songs are more adroit and cleverly sophisticated than spontaneous. Although the latter part of this statement especially should be accepted with a fair amount of diffidence, the over-all meaning (to the extent any generality can be worthy) is true. One of Chausson's chief merits, in this respect, is that, in his "fastidious discrimination," his *Mélodies* always bask in an atmosphere of sincerity that is not hampered by precious refinement. There is nothing "clever" about them, and whatever sophistication there may be stems directly from their author's natural aristocratic attributes. His ubiquitous effort towards a self-contained idiom that would express in music only music itself has succeeded generally in attributing to text, tune, and accompaniment coequal roles, as the form demands. It was his chief concern never to allow his style to leap out of bounds and never to strain the idea or feeling it translated. For this reason Chausson hated all forms of artifice, whose prime besetting fault is to resort to external ornaments and pompous dramatic devices.

Not all the *Mélodies,* however, are of equal value. At first, it is surprising to discover the wide gap of difference that separates certain pieces of almost prohibitive complexity, like *Serre chaude* (from *Serres chaudes*), from others of inviting simplicity, like *La dernière feuille.* Upon closer analysis, it becomes apparent that usually the complexity arises from the obscuration imposed by overintricate accompaniments and

[2] McKinney and Anderson, *Music in History,* 656.

Ernest Chausson

not necessarily from a confused harmonic context. We also note, from the chronology of the opus numbers, how consistently the evolution mounts from the simple to the complex. The plainness of Chausson's early opera, written around the early 1880's—the gentle fluttering of *Les Papillons* (Opus 2, No. 3) or the easy fluidity of *Sérénade italienne* (Opus 2, No. 5)—gives way gradually to the greater intricacy of the *Sérénade* (Opus 13, No. 2) and *L'Aveu* (Opus 13, No. 3), in which an unmistakable thickening of the piano accompaniments with cross rhythms, arpeggios, and uneasy modulations is evident. The *Serres chaudes* (Opus 24), finally, allow but rare moments of calm and relaxation, as the texture becomes so heavy that it has been described as an "unrelieved elegiac atmosphere." But then, as if suffering himself from fatigue, Chausson relaxes in the ease of the *Trois lieder* (Opus 27), where "the cosmic questionings and the sense of frustrated emotion are forgotten" and where he returns "to a happier, clearer emotional world and a correspondingly cleaner palette."[3]

Chausson is not to blame completely for the heavy musical drapery which hangs behind the thin melodies of the *Serres chaudes*. If it is true that a piano-voice melody is above all a *"genre charmant,"* which requires the luminous body of thought in the text to shine through the accompaniment and that therefore the scope of the harmonic design should be reduced to the limited potential of the pianoforte to preserve the essential beauty of the genre, it is equally true that harmonic complexity and the expansive feeling of polyphonic development are best suited to the needs of the subject matter

[3] Martin Cooper, *French Music*, 63.

His Works: The Mélodies

of these particular texts. For the *Serres chaudes,* as the musical setting of Maurice Maeterlinck's dream-ridden poems, had to express the haunts of mystery and the vague fears before the unknown that characterize the text: moments of weariness and ennui, of sadness, of fever, of prayer. True to his ideal, Chausson's accompanimental background has discarded any suggestion of plastic description and tried to bring out the various indistinct feelings by elaborating every possible harmonic detail.

In the first *Serre,* for example (*"O serre au milieu des forêts..."*), though not a superior composition—possibly due to the incoherence of the text, Chausson did not try to reproduce the forest, the postilion's call, or the *"musique de cuivre,"* realizing that their only value resides in the feeling they materialize. Hence the agitated piano in B-minor with passing modulations. In view of the abstruseness of the text, we cannot say that the bursts of musical movement are completely justified; yet the final stanza, which is musically translatable, is wonderfully rendered: *"Quand aurons-nous la pluie"* is a gem of melody standing out over expressive harmonies.

Serre d'ennui, whose text is simpler and more sober, receives a more elegant treatment than the bulk of the preceding one. *Fauves las* with its many modulations, *Lassitude* with its harmonies which toll like knells and without pause, and *Oraison,* truly the best of the *Serres,* with its soothing religious flow composed of the same harmonies which concluded the setting of the first poem, are ample evidence that the composer is not merely a delicate musician but also an equally delicate literary interpreter. It might seem that the vocal line makes no pretense at melodic continuity, but ac-

Ernest Chausson

tually it is aiming at a faithful rendition of the finer feelings behind the words and remaining within the framework of pure music. The result of this technique is most satisfactory; it interprets the text without making it any heavier in its general ennui than it already is. There is an indirect sense of suffering in this music, the suffering of a man who cannot escape from the narrow prison chamber of his individual self. In this metaphysics lies the secret of its appeal. Debussy praised the *Serres* highly when he said: "These melodies are little dramas with an impassioned metaphysics; Chausson's music comments it without making it dull. One would even wish that he had given more freedom to all the palpitations of inner emotion that one hears in his very personal musical interpretation."[4]

Like Hugo Wolf, it seems that Chausson cherished the idea of composing cycles of songs from the works of various poets: Verlaine, Leconte de Lisle, Gautier, Maeterlinck, Shakespeare, Mauclair, etc. Frequently, and possibly for reasons of friendship, he collaborated with Maurice Bouchor, who literarily was not in the same class as the others, but whose verses express the tender and nostalgic simplicity of a fading love emotion, a theme that appealed greatly to Chausson's artistic temperament. With the exception of *Le Temps des Lilas,* however, the results of this direct collaboration were less successful than those of his indirect union with the better poets. There are elegant contrapuntal rhythms in both *Nocturne* (Opus 8, No. 1) and *Nos souvenirs* (Opus 8, No. 4), the latter actually serving as a musical reminiscence of the former, but the commonplace expression of a past love seems

[4] Quoted from Léon Vallas, *Les Idées de Claude Debussy,* 70.

122

His Works: The Mélodies

to chill slightly the musical conception of *Amour d'Antan* (Opus 8, No. 2) and *Printemps triste* (Opus 8, No. 3), despite the warm feeling infused into the latter by the composer's agitated piano accompaniment.

Le Temps des Lilas, on the contrary, is a masterpiece of grace and delicacy. Strictly speaking, it is an extract from the moving *Poème de l'Amour et de la Mer,* in which the voice is seconded by an orchestral accompaniment of rare and absorbing amplitude. The theme of *Le Temps* pervades the entire work in cyclic fashion, appearing variously in the accompaniment, constituting the orchestral interlude, and emerging as the final song, where the accompaniment, recalling the interlude, seems to suffice by itself, somewhat like that of Fauré's *Clair de lune.* But whereas the *Poème de l'Amour et de la Mer* suffers slightly from its unrelieved tone of declamation and from occasional prolixity in the developments, *Le Temps,* constituting its closing section with a final statement of the haunting D minor theme,

Lent et triste

EXAMPLE I

is a fine entity in itself and is justifiably included in the collections of the *Mélodies.*

Bouchor's verses have a quality of resigned simplicity, quite reminiscent of the most tender sonnets by Pierre de Ronsard. *"Notre fleur d'amour est si bien fanée"* echoes the sixteenth-century poet's *"Languissante, elle meurt, feuille à*

123

feuille déclose."[5] It is like a nostalgia of death; its mortal melancholy is ably rendered by Chausson's minor tonality, syncopated movement in the accompaniment, and caressing instances of punctuation, such as the exquisite modulation from D minor to D Major that occurs at the end of the fourth verse.

Closely resembling *Le Temps des Lilas,* both with respect to mood and rhythm, is *Les Heures,* an evocative interpretation of Mauclair's vague and obscure lyrics. There is less movement in this number, chiefly because the melodic line never wanders far away from the dominant tone "A" (this melody too is in D minor), with the result that the text itself acquires greater significance and the music conveys a wanted feeling of resignation, notwithstanding the obsessive harmonic indecisions produced by an obstinate pedal point. About it Mauclair himself declared: "How his music has prolonged my poor words! How he has enriched with all his genius this humble, little plaint, and how powerful the music is!"[6] The other two melodies constituting the *Trois lieder* (Opus 27), *Ballade* and *Les Couronnes,* are equally deserving of special mention. The greatest charm of *Ballade* stems from the contrary rhythms dominating the first part of the poem which speaks in separate images of angel's wings and ship's sails, and from the more agitated ending with its downward arpeggios which seem to flutter elegantly, like flapping wings or sails in the wind, around the two combined images. In *Les Couronnes,* Chausson tried to parallel the gracious naïveté of the text by adopting the free gait of a popular song. To be

---

[5] *"Comme on voit sur la branche," Les Amours de Marie,* II, 4.
[6] Mauclair, *La Religion de la Musique,* 74.

His Works: The Mélodies

sure, however, his "popular song" exhibits careful workmanship and a rich flow of nuances. "These . . . melodies are perfect in form and possess an inexactness which contrasts with the feeling of definiteness that the older lieder by the same composer express."[7]

Verlaine, as we have mentioned, was the most genuine representative of his generation, and a poet from whose works Chausson would have drawn more and more, we feel sure, if his lifetime had been longer. It is not surprising to discover that, despite the small share this poet has in the composer's copious song production, the musical settings of *Apaisement, La Chanson bien douce,* and *Le Chevalier Malheur* are of unequaled purity. In no other *Mélodie* is Chausson more a poet's musician. Debussy himself, who made a most successful and more extensive use of Verlaine, is not any gentler nor is he any more perceptively delicate than Chausson.

We are even tempted to state that Debussy can be said to paint, however subtly, with the solid pigments of oil colors, whereas Chausson uses his brush to apply the soft shades of water colors, and *Aquarelles*[8] is actually more in keeping with the translucent mood of the Parisian poet. What lends itself more characteristically to Chausson's temperament than the following verses found in *La Chanson bien douce?*

> . . . . *rien n'est meilleur à l'âme*
> *Que de faire une âme moins triste.*
> *Elle est en peine et de passage*
> *L'âme qui souffre sans colère.* . . .

[7] Georges Servières, *"Lieder français, Ernest Chausson," Le Guide Musical,* No. 7 (December 19, 1897), 843–46.

[8] Section in Verlaine's *Romances sans paroles,* n. p.

Ernest Chausson

In its attention to minute detail and in its mature delicacy, the music has some of the feeling of a Pre-Raphaelite painting. The moving chromaticism of the accompaniment along with the frequent warm stress of low notes catch the strange perfume of the poetry. The over-all effect is as satisfying as Debussy's setting of Verlaine's *Green;* we feel as great a sense of polish and precision in literary understanding.

The song to which Chausson gave the title of *Apaisement* is even more striking, perhaps because of the difficulty posed by the nature of Verlaine's text. There is nothing complicated, nothing claiming the distinction of perceptive thought. The poem is like a murmur, the murmur of a slow dream that analyzes a semiconscious, semi-ecstatic emotion. It has tempted many musicians, but none has rendered it more exquisitely. In order to reconcile the fundamental nature of music, which is movement, and the unmoving, lingering quality of the poem, Chausson has founded the whole accompaniment on a few gentle chords hovering about the E minor tonality in which they resolve themselves unnoticed, almost mysteriously, after each modulation. With *Le Chevalier Malheur,* written after *La Chanson bien douce* in 1898, the composer wrote his third and last interpretation of Verlaine. The poem is a real notation of emotive language, and the musical setting follows its changing moods with feverish delicacy, from the symbolism of the objects described to the phantom-like appearance of the knight to the inspiriting quality of his words. It is a gem of tone-colored interpretation, beginning in an inquisitive C♯ minor and ending in a resigned, almost fatigued but not disconsolate F Major. The poetico-musical elements of rhythm and timber, undistinguished in each drift of expressed emotion, create something resembling Chausson himself: one feels his presence.

Occasionally, Chausson abandoned himself to richly lyrical feelings, in response either to an emotional demand (*"Le Colibri"* by Leconte de Lisle) or to a dramatic demand (*"La Caravane"* by Théophile Gautier) of the text. *Le Colibri,* with its unusual 5/4 rhythm and its almost Italian feeling for the voice, has become one of his best-known songs. It belongs to the first period of the composer's output, the Opus 2 (1882), which contains perhaps his most charming numbers. Its steady chord accompaniment, quite conventional in nature, with a melodic superposition alternating between voice and piano, gives way at the climax to eight measures of rolling, broken chords, and then returns to the original chord device. The effect is one of simplicity, architectural balance, and rare beauty. One would wish, however, that the relationship between music and text had been closer, for Chausson placed a musical climax where the poem does not call for it. But the whole is redeemed by the simplicity of his treatment of the poem, which describes the flight and death of a hummingbird, and by capturing, in its final movement, the analogy between the bird and the poet's soul through a meaningful recapitulation.

In *La Caravane,* however, the correspondence between physical situation and musical expression is both fine and strong. Instead of a simple *mélodie,* it is rather a symphonic poem, as one critic has labeled it.[9] In fact, an orchestrated version by the composer himself exists. The work does have

[9] Servières, *"Lieder français, Ernest Chausson,"* Le Guide Musical, No. 7 (December 19, 1897), 843–46.

great instrumental possibilities with its sudden dynamic shifts that range from a "ff" to a "pp" or its dominating crescendo-decrescendo pattern that transcribes the slow trudge of a tired caravan. "The conclusion, which modulates from E minor to E Major by means of the simplest chords, creates the impression of melancholic serenity that befits the verses of Théophile Gautier."[10] *La Caravane* is weightier and more declamatory than the typical Chausson song, but the highly imagistic quality of the text warrants it. The vocal exposition would seem to border on the recitative, though this might be due more to its chromaticism—a chromaticism that is strongly suggestive of Wagner—than to its linear conception.

Unusual, indeed, are the four *Chansons de Shakespeare* (Opus 28) set to Maurice Bouchor's translations. They revolve hauntingly around themes of a forlorn love or a bemoaned death, each with a peculiar "passed" quality, passed in time and in hope. The *Chanson de Clown* from *Twelfth Night* rings with a declamation that could almost be considered operatic. It is spleen at its most acute, but it is far from desperately revealed. The prevailing sadness of the E minor mode in the phrase *"Fuis, mon âme"* is compensated by the resigned courage of the line *". . . que nul ami . . . n'ait des paroles de douleur,"* a feeling which finds musical corroboration in occasional major triads in the slow accompaniment.

Somewhat similar is the *Chanson d'amour* from *Measure for Measure,* except that the abandoned lover's impossible dream of reward (*"Mais si malgré tout ma douleur te touche"*) is heightened dramatically by a panting accompaniment in high register before the inevitable subsiding of the

[10] *Ibid.*

His Works: The Mélodies

final verse *"En vain . . ."* Then the *Chanson d'Ophélie* from *Hamlet,* brief and touching, discloses more poignantly the mood of something passed, as the bereaved heroine likens "his" death to that of the thousand flowers which, before having followed "him" to the grave, have drunk the tears of a sincere love. Musically, this exquisite thought never allows the pain it engenders to be translated in vulgar movements. This is Chausson at his serenest.

Finally, there is the *Chant funèbre* from *Much Ado About Nothing* for a four-voice women's chorus. The original piano accompaniment was later effectively orchestrated by Vincent d'Indy. Again the "passed" quality emerges to the surface, this time stylistically, leaving a subtle impression of pervasive, suffused modality. Each voice, horizontally conceived, shares in the general effect by its independence rather than by its vertical relation to the other voices. The whole, then, is contrapuntal rather than harmonic. There is no overcrowding, no redundance or lack of clarity; on the contrary, the balance is admirable, beginning in *a cappella* fashion and increasing its intensity as the accompaniment corroborates more and more the movement of the voices, maintaining throughout its unyielding contrapuntal intent. The result, someone has commented, is "one of the most tragic and poignant deplorations that the thought of death has ever inspired in music."[11]

Perhaps one of the most striking examples of Chausson's noted *"tristesse,"* in this case the kind that borders on bitter despair, is his Opus 37, the *Chanson perpétuelle,* a veritable

[11] Hallays, *"Le Roi Arthus," Revue de Paris,* Vol. VI (December 15, 1903), 852.

musical poem on the verses of Charles Cros. Scored for single piano or mixed (orchestra or piano-string quartet) accompaniment, the instrumental portion looms equal in value with the vocal, confidently underlining the text with its noble symphonic quality. The verses, though not very original, as the title suggests, are eloquent, and the music finds no difficulty in commenting on them with equal eloquence, modulating frequently and varying its rhythmic patterns around the theme

EXAMPLE 2

which also closes the song with what is one of the most beautiful endings Chausson ever penned. Without doubt, the *Chanson perpétuelle* is one of the compositions that leaves in our mouths the desire to savor his subsequent works, a desire which we know must remain unfulfilled, for the song was written in 1898, less than one year before his death. By this time, his musical idea had been magnified, having gained effectively in simplicity together with assurance, solidity, and ampleness. Correspondingly, in this song, his emotion is less elusive, the flavor of the *"pays lointain"* of isolation immediately recognizable, and the musical impulse nourished to maturity.

The year before the *Chanson perpétuelle,* Chausson wrote his Opus 36, that is, the *Cantique à l'épouse* and the popular *Dans la Forêt du charme et de l'enchantement,* both very dif-

Chausson with Eugène Ysaÿe

ferent from the *Chanson*. Under Albert Jounet's canticle he placed an unassuming accompaniment: Schubertian, let us say, in rhythm, early Debussyan in harmony—a successful combination to bring out the mood of the poetry's

> *Viens me chanter un cantique*
> *Beau comme une sombre rose*
> *Ou plutôt ne chante pas*
> *Viens te coucher sur mon coeur....*

The second song, on verses by Jean Moréas, is wonderfully fleeting and volatile in quality, like the dream of the golden scepter offered by the gnome. Yet the relaxed, rolling musical background is persistent—as persistent as the dreamer's desire to sleep in the enchanted forest: *"Qu'importe si je sais que c'est mirage et leurre."* The effortlessness of these two settings by Chausson makes the compositions singularly appealing. Better still, the poems are made more luring and absorbing by this quality. During his last years, it seems, the composer's simplicity and equanimity of treatment, reached in the abandonment of calmness, are a mature echo of the early opera *Nanny, Le Charme, Les Papillons,* and *La dernière feuille.*

Opus 11 appears under the title *Deux Duos, La Nuit* by Théodore de Banville, and *Le Réveil* by Honoré de Balzac. Here Chausson is at his simplest, perhaps due to the serenity of the texts he has chosen. Banville's "fresh kiss" of night and the intoxicating "perfume of the air," devoid of cares and troubles, combine musically in the compelling invitation of the *"Repose-toi"* under the shimmering light of the stars. Its descent seems to be translated by the constant downward movement of the accompaniment, usually in moving arpeggios and sometimes in the form of single notes acting like brief sparks of sound, as it were, punctuating the silence. In the *Réveil,* as in the *Nuit,* the two voices enjoy complete independence but retain at all times their mutual agreement. Balzac's poem is fashioned after the romances that were so much in vogue during his day, but what a difference of musical inspiration between this and the banal setting by Auber of the romance in *Modeste Mignon!* Here the music, far superior to the text, establishes a haunting, religious, bell-like mood, moving comfortably from one tonality to another, giving way to a faster middle section that emphasizes the first beat of every measure, and concluding with a return to the "bell" motive in variation form. Over this backdrop, the two voices are clearly outlined. Someone has said of this number: "It exasperates itself in a movement of intense life, and evokes warmly the happiness promised during the day, from morning time, to those who wake with love in their hearts."[12] Beginning calmly in the middle register, it rises progressively into the sunshine.

Finally, there are the *Chansons de Miarka,* Opus 17, two poems by Jean Richepin which attracted Chausson and which he improved by the quality of his musical setting. On the whole, they rely on his double affinity for contained descriptiveness and simple pathos. The first of these, *Les Morts,* is an interesting example of how a song based on death need not sound somber or lugubrious at all. The composer retains a fitting minor tonality, but so many are the transitions to

[12] Adrien Remacle *"Mélodies et Mélodistes," La Mode Pratique,* October, 1895.

His Works: The Mélodies

major chords that any atmosphere of gloom is immediately cleared. In this way, he is able to reach the true meaning of the key phrase, "The dead will live," which is symbolized later in the passage of a kiss from one mouth to another. The second, *La Pluie,* is a light description of rain on dead leaves, on dust and on grain, lyrical, to be sure, but not without a dainty dose of capriciousness. Appropriately, the piano accompaniment moves along steadily and delicately in a gladsome rustle. Because of its mood, however, *La Pluie* is less characteristic of the composer than *Les Morts,* and whereas its unusual Grieglike melody may lure us, some of us may feel less attracted to a number that does not allow us to sense the secrets of Chausson's musical personality as we have sensed it elsewhere.

This musical personality, then, as we have endeavored to show through the *Mélodies,* speaks to us personally with its compelling attraction of tenderness and melancholy, and most of all with its engaging, soft-hued directness, as in the youthful and fresh pages of *Hébé, Nanny, L'Apaisement,* or even of the simple *La Cigale.* These are compositions whose grace and expressiveness equal the melodic breadth of the best in Fauré and Duparc. These are also compositions which lay bare the soul that he is to conceal slightly in subsequent works under the thin veil of his *"pudeur,"* his scrupulosity, the naturally aristocratic containment of his philosophical lamentations. When, later, his longer works will become of necessity more impassioned and weighty, none of the taste for measure and persistent feeling for simplicity of the *Mélodies* will be lost. The *Mélodies* mark Chausson's personality. For its essence was melody, the vocal or instrumental melody

Ernest Chausson

that laments but never moans, dreams but never exaggerates, prays but never implores. If at times he is not a minute musical translator of the poet's text, he is always an interpreter by virtue of the emotions and remembrances that the poems awaken in his heart. His interpretations exude, on the one hand, a desire for freedom, and on the other, a sense of solitariness, characteristics that often, while remaining faithful to the basic idea of the text, add imperceptible modifications which eventually make us feel the presence of the composer more than the poet. They are noble, yet they never claim to outrange us; rather they abide discreetly by our side, never excessively insistent, awaiting our meditation to enhance the enduring emotions they utter.

Religious Music

THE outstanding feature about Chausson's religious music is its impersonalism. This means that it has that detached quality necessary to invest a prayer of a service with the elevation owed to the religious thought, and not with the admiration which attracts the worshiper to the personality of the composer. Even in *La Légende de Sainte Cécile,* the impersonalism of what we could rightly consider apart as a religious number, the *Cantique de Cécile,* is quite different from, say, the celebrated Ave Marias of Schubert, Gounod, and Verdi. It is in this music that Chausson's ability to abstract himself becomes most evident.

Opus 31, *Les Vêpres des Vierges* (actually the ninth series of *Les Vêpres du Commun des Saints*) is a most attractive example of this abstraction. It is comprised of eight sections of varying length, each with an appropriate organ anthem, and is followed by three other brief anthems for the Magnificat. The theme from the first section, *"Haec est virgo Sapiens et una"* (*calme,* 5/4, D minor) is a good example of how the composer has captured the pure, liturgical flavor of the service:

Ernest Chausson

EXAMPLE 3

There follow: the second, *"Haec est virgo Sapiens, quam Dominus"* (*sans lenteur*, 6/4, D minor); the third, *"Hae est quae nescivit"* (*sans lenteur*, 3/4, C♯ minor); the fourth, *"Veni electa mea"* (*lent*, 4/4, D minor); the fifth, *"Ista est speciosa"* (*sans lenteur*, 3/4, C♯ minor); the sixth, (*"a magnificat"*): *"Veni Sponsa Christi"* (*sans lenteur*, 7/8, A Major); the seventh, *"Prudentes Virgines"* (*modéré*, 12/8, C Major); and the eighth, again *"Veni Sponsa Christi"* (*modéré*, 3/2, G Major).

To be noted are the second, with its parallel harmonic texture; the third, with the broken chords upholding a sustained, single melody note in higher register; the fifth, with its engulfing movement:

EXAMPLE 4

the sixth, with its pronounced organ quality and the movement of its 7/8 tempo; and the contrapuntal seventh above

136

all, with its rolling arpeggio movement under the melody, giving way eventually to the block-chord structure of the opening, and the impressive, grandiose "fortissimo" ending.

Chausson's *Pater Noster* is strange; it is the strangeness that must be heard twice to be appreciated. The whole prayer seems to hang together on a few dissonances, many modulations to major keys, and the *"fiat voluntas"* phrase which appears later in the accompaniment as well as in the voice. It is also strange because of its feminine pureness and the resultant incongruity which listeners might sense, due to its dedication to the Almighty Father. Yet, despite the curious flavor in the listener's ear, it lingers quietly noble and all-absorbing.

More direct is the *Ave Verum Corpus* (Opus 6, No. 2) for voice with harmonium accompaniment. Built along more conventional lines of hymnology, with only occasional yielding to chromatic devices, it is not difficult to explain its appeal and the popularity which has made it a short solo number for various instruments. The initial theme (*pas trop lent*) in E Major is carried with great regularity of movement for twenty-five measures until a very expressive middle section (*un peu plus vite*), only to return and frame the hymn on the last page where a fine effect is achieved by resolving a minor tonality into a final *"tierce de Picardie"* closing chord. Striking also is the way in which a very contained climax towards the end infuses this musical prayer with a heightened religious tone.

Perhaps the most beautiful page of Chausson's religious music is his *Tota pulchra es, Maria,* for voice and accompaniment. Its religious inspiration rings with lovely truth. The composer seems to be more at home when singing to the Virgin. With the same liturgical objectivity and lack of pomp which mark all his religious numbers, the *Tota pulchra* is nevertheless warmer and, by the same token, more devout. Its wonderful opening phrase

EXAMPLE 5

is almost a reverse of the 'cello passage in the *Cantique de Cécile,* and is carried through the composition with the tranquillity appropriate for the *Virgo clementissima.* Nothing can be cleaner than his accompaniment, nothing more entrancing than his modulations which rise and settle softly to leave us finally with the impression that we have heard not a simple prayer to the Blessed Mother but a psalm of lingering, extolling beauty.

At one time, Chausson decided to make use of a solo child's voice over a four-voice mixed choir and organ accompaniment. For this combination he wrote an *Ave Maria* (in E Major), whose theme is not too far removed from some of those quoted above:

EXAMPLE 6

His Works: Religious Music

First stated by the organ, it then passes to the solo voice and is returned by the organ in arpeggio development, and at the Sancta Maria the whole choir joins. The mounting effect, even if obvious, is not without interest, especially when abetted by frequent chord changes. A 'cello has sometimes substituted the solo voice in performances.

The composer also used a multiple combination in his *Lauda, Sion, Salvatorem,* Opus 16, No. 1, in G, a motet for soprano (or tenor) with violin, organ, and harp accompaniment. Because it contains nothing to hint at an emotional climax and very little harmonic variation (the effects are due more to the interplay between violin and voice than to anything else), we are, in this case, not too pleased before the flat flavor of this kind of simplicity and restraint. We receive the same impression from two other works, the solemn *Deus Abraham* in A and the very proper *Tantum Ergo Sacramentum* in G, both for voice with organ and violin accompaniment, the latter with harp also.

In summary, then, we should select four numbers whereby Chausson shows us that in religious music, too, he is a composer of rare attainment: the *Prudentes Virgines* from the *Vêpres du Commun des Vierges,* the *Ave Verum Corpus,* and the *Tota pulchra es, Maria.* Along with them we should not fail to mention also the magnificent *Cantique de Cécile* in *La Légende de Sainte Cécile,* to be discussed in a later chapter. These are pages of dramatic import as well as of simple, direct appeal, of liturgical plainness as well as of lyrical elevation. Different as they may be from one another, a serene reserve—the only trace of the composer's presence—envelops all of them.

Chamber Music

" CHAUSSON pondered at length over his works before writing them down, and touched them up meticulously afterward. For Chausson belonged to the strong race of those who suffer through their idea before producing it."[1] D'Indy's words may be applied characteristically to the Trio in G minor, the Concert in D Major, the Piano Quartet in A Major, and the Quartet in C minor, each of which responds to a strong determination for sound musical construction, sometimes satisfactorily or at other times imperfectly realized. The *Mélodies* brought to light the sensitive personality; the chamber works, more genuinely than his dramatic and symphonic music, illustrate the artist. Certainly the Piano Quartet is his art at its most successful and powerful. From the Trio, Opus 3, to the latter composition, Opus 30, the development from a richly endowed scholar to a master is immediately traceable.

The Trio in G minor for pianoforte, violin, and violoncello was composed in 1881 when, unsatisfied with his progress under Jules Massenet, Chausson went to work under César Franck. In fact, it would be difficult to find in it any

[1] Vincent d'Indy, *La Tribune de Saint-Gervais*, September, 1899.

distinctly Massenetian language, and, if anything, the opus as a whole makes it easy for us to understand his choice of the Belgian musician, about whom Debussy was to say later: "His is a disinterested reverie which does not allow itself any sighs whose veracity it has not experienced beforehand."[2] The first movement, consisting of a short twenty-nine measure introduction (*pas trop lent*) and an allegro (marked *animé*), is very stirring with its chromaticism and intricate piano texture into which is blended the restlessness of sudden dynamic changes. It clings almost desperately to one theme:

EXAMPLE 7

to which all other ideas concur, as if afraid to stray from it. No less despair—perhaps we should say angry resignation —marks its final statements and the conclusion of the movement.

The second movement, an intermezzo (*vite*), is weaker. We should guess from it that Chausson was less at ease when handling fast rhythms. The rigid three or four-measure rhythms in an unyielding 3/8 tempo could only depend on interesting thematic material to carry them through. This, however, is not the case. A too strict adherence to symmetry

[2] Léon Vallas, *Les Idées de Claude Debussy*, 67.

forces the composer to write otherwise avoidable double-stops for the violin, while elsewhere some of the harmonic difficulties inherent in the structure itself are solved by plain open fourths, fifths, and octaves. Yet the piano part is not without an element of wit.

The third movement is an andante (*assez lent*), a wonderfully luring expansion of a first movement idea:

EXAMPLE 8

With such a theme, both plaintive and pure, Chausson is at home, for his cognizance of the sonorous potential of each note is exact, using all tones with the kind of precision that never requires of them what they do not contain. Furthermore, the three instruments each retain their expressive individuality while finely joined to give utterance to their common mood.

In the fourth and finale movement (*animé*), there is much which betrays the new follower of César Franck: the running chromaticism, the cyclical return of a previous theme (even if a mere echo in this case), the developing intensity of the whole movement, and its general solidity of structure. Despite some prolixity and a few ameliorable passages, this whole final section of the Trio sparkles with variety—thematic and, on occasion, rhythmical—and concludes a musical essay devoted, perhaps primarily, to exercising the skills of good craftsmanship and inspirational conciseness. About the

His Works: Chamber Music

Trio, D'Indy was to write: "One feels, amidst beauties and weaknesses, aspirations as yet unrealized of his soul, foreshadowing future works."[3]

Obviously satisfied with the inspired tutelage of César Franck, Chausson wrote between 1889–91 the Concert in D Major, Opus 21, for pianoforte, violin, and string quartet. The critic K. S. Sorabji calls it "one of the most original and beautiful chamber works of modern times."[4] In truth, all the themes, meticulously chosen, are of uncontestable artistic merit and are treated with a mature perspective that distinguishes this composition most favorably from the preceding Opus 3. Eugene Ysaÿe, to whom the work is dedicated and who played the solo violin part at its first performance in Brussels in 1892, was delighted by it, and his trusting appreciation did much to give Chausson the self-confidence he needed when working at the chamber genre. As Sorabji correctly points out, one is invariably reminded of an eighteenth-century *concerto grosso,* a Bach *Brandenburg Concerto,* with its *concertanti* instruments. The impressive feature is Chausson's treatment of all component parts: both solo instruments, even when used antiphonally or as duettists, are granted a rare freedom and breadth of development which in no way interfere with the generous lines along which the quartet proceeds, but which at the same time draw from their pervading quality all necessary sustenance and support.

A detailed analysis of the first movement will show us the careful mechanics of Chausson's composing technique.

[3] "Ernest Chausson," *Cobbett's Cyclopedic Survey of Chamber Music,* 266.

[4] Kaikhosru Shapurji Sorabji, *Mi Contra Fa,* 120.

Ernest Chausson

The fundamental three-note theme is stated by the pianoforte in the opening measures of a thirty-four measure introduction or preparation:

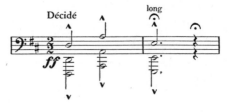

EXAMPLE 9

It is immediately reinforced by the quartet, under which the piano functions decoratively. After the preparation, a burst of melody by the solo violin, an expansion of the three-note theme into the beautifully noble and lyrical subject of the movement:

EXAMPLE 10

The piano supports the melody as in a violin-piano sonata before the entrance of the quartet repeating the theme energetically.

Then, we are introduced to a second theme, derived from the first and written for the solo violin, doubled by the violoncello and developed at some length. Four bars of *calme* inter-

rupt the movement's *animé* with a piano motive, followed by
two short melodic units chiefly for the solo violin, the first
recalling the second theme, the second foreshadowing, as the
piano had done, the third. This is stated in full by the solo
violin over complete accompaniment:

EXAMPLE II

until a resolute intervention of the three-note figure by 'cello
and viola. The 'cello then picks up the main theme in G
Major and is echoed shortly afterward by the first violin. In
turn, the solo violin transforms it into a rhythmic variant,
quickly making its way into the piano part under the now
decorative violin. Theme two is then treated by the viola and
'cello, subsequently by the solo violin, and is exposed at some
length before being forcefully dominated by the three-note
figure with all instruments playing in unison. Before a short
cadenza passage, the solo violin develops the third theme,
then joins the piano in a recapitulation of the first theme;
after a fifteen-bar interlude dominated by the piano, con-
secutive returns of the third subject, of the principal subject,
and of the ever punctuating three-note figure, bring to a close
a highly successful piece of writing, both moving and dreamy,
penetrated by the double action of persuasive statement and
fleeting charm.

Also very effective is the second movement, a Sicilienne

in A minor (*pas vite*). Actually, it is built wholly on the single lulling melody:

EXAMPLE 12

despite the variety offered by a second motive appearing after the twenty-eighth measure. This motive is used contrapuntally with the main theme thereafter. The movement is of imaginative tenderness, or, as D'Indy described it, like the "charming fanciful gardens of Gabriel Fauré."[5]

Third movement, a *grave* in D minor, is largely a mood description, rather foreboding and fatefully resigned in character. It is a typical Chausson writing here, the composer of the Symphony's "Largo" movement or the farewells in *Le Roi Arthus*. A chromatic opening introduces the main subject with the solo violin, slowly giving way to the second subject, whose melody and rhythm produce what are possibly some of the most anguish-stricken pages in chamber-music literature:

EXAMPLE 13

[5] "Ernest Chausson," *Cobbett's Cyclopedic Survey of Chamber Music,* I, 267.

The ominous first theme returns paraphrased at the end in a gigantic climax, a full-fledged despair bearing none of the accents of hope that give breath to Beethoven's sufferings. The final subsiding in F minor, with its returning chromatic figure, is like a settlement in death. Recalling Alexis de Castillon's and Guillaume Lekeu's early deaths, one could ask with D'Indy how much of this was premonition on Chausson's part.

Finally, the last movement, the finale (*très animé*), is perhaps more interesting than successful. It contains essentially one idea:

EXAMPLE 14

treated in variation rather than in sonata form: little development as such and mostly rhythmic amplification or abbreviation. Though chiefly in D minor, the D Major tonality, altogether unheard since the first movement, makes brief reappearances, especially at the very end, to justify the title of the work. About halfway through the movement we again hear the previous movement's theme briefly but vigorously restated, after which the composer continues to toy with his original idea and concludes the otherwise fine work with a long, little effective coda. It betrays what could have been his

Ernest Chausson

mental fatigue. After having penned the last measure, Chausson himself was to have exclaimed: "Another failure!" (*"Encore une oeuvre ratée!"*).

Notwithstanding his self-critical remark, we must conclude for ourselves that the Concert is a meritorious contribution to the chamber-music repertory. If only for the distinctive beauty and refinement of his melodic ideas, the work is striking; it was not without reason that Octave Maus passionately referred to it in 1892 when defending the art of the "younger generation."

The culminating point of Chausson's career in chamber-music writing is undoubtedly the Piano Quartet in A Major, Opus 30, for pianoforte, violin, viola, and violoncello. Here is a work of real depth, lofty inspiration, and pure form. With fresh ideas, such as the cyclic treatment of thematic material and its rhythmic modifications, the whole architecture is strengthened and enriched. Furthermore, in this work, Chausson shows he has learned the skill of putting given phrases through a series of subtle transfigurations, a knowledge which greatly enhances the intellectual range of the opus. Though the basic melancholic features of the *Mélodies* again set the mood for the new work, we should be wrong in searching for evidence of true sadness or even resignation. On the contrary, the Piano Quartet seems to exude surprising confidence, the unmistakable sign of an artist's attained maturity.

The first movement (*animé*) begins with a strongly marked exposition of the main theme, strongly oriental in flavor:

148

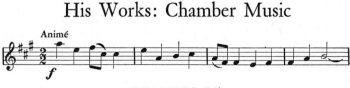

EXAMPLE 15

This subject is then broken down into two constituents, one rhythmic, the other melodic, and guided through varied modulations to the key of C (with flat in the seventh) in which the second theme is stated:

EXAMPLE 16[6]

[6] A glance at Chausson's sketchbook from 1896 on is interesting: it reveals a never completed number for oboe, viola, piano, and string quartet, at the beginning of which the piano theme is almost identical with the above theme in the Piano Quartet:

EXAMPLE 17

149

Ernest Chausson

Next comes a long, 159-bar development section, beginning with a restatement of the main theme, a rhythmical explanation of it as well as of the second subject, gradually brought into the open through the key of D to a clear C♯ minor. The recapitulation occurs normally, with the second theme more extended than before and resolving in a *"plus calme"* section scored in F Major. Finally, the last seventy-two bars of the movement are devoted to the coda or final development, in which the first theme reappears by augmentation, then by change of rhythm from 2/2 to 6/4 with the concomitant return to the original key of A. A fading reminiscence of the second subject brings the movement to a lovely close.

To designate the second movement (*très calme*) with words short of superlatives would be risking injustice. The lied theme around which it is erected is one of Chausson's most beautiful melodic inspirations, haunting and tender, captivating and sorrowful despite its D-flat Major tonality. The viola introduces it:

EXAMPLE 18

After only forty measures, a new phrase is set up in the key of F. During the course of its long development, it winds its way through a maze of modulations, wavelike in nature, each flowing onto the other and injecting thereby a touch of restlessness into the pervading calm. Then, agogically developed through successive suggestions, the first subject returns, and, at the height of a climactic crescendo, is declaimed triumphantly by the pianoforte in D flat. The movement dims quickly thereafter into a vanishing C♯ minor conclusion. So simple and so appealing, so consummately written, this second section of the Piano Quartet is endowed with the rare quality of possessing a magnificent melody that lends itself at the same time to chamber-music requirements of development.

The main theme of the third movement (*simple et sans hâte*) resembles somewhat the first subject of the first move-

EXAMPLE 19

ment, as a melodic inversion with slight rhythmic alteration. Thematically it seems to be constructed on some folk song with the D tonality dominating, from minor in the beginning to major in the end. Never is the mood lost, even during the second section. It is, on the contrary, impressed upon us by means of a lengthy return to the first subject, in rhythmic variation and a bit more restless, but always unyielding in its obstinate, leisurely pace.

Again in the fourth movement (*animé*) we may say that the first theme is derived from a previously used idea. In this case, notwithstanding the agitated 6/8-time mood in A minor, the preceding movement is recalled. After the exposition, a modulatory link gradually leads the section to a calmer D flat in which the second subject is at first outlined by the pianoforte, then stated by the strings in a beautifully ascending phrase. With the value of each note doubled, the lied theme of the second movement glimmers echo-like, but briefly, from the violin; the real second theme of the finale of the Piano Quartet is little more than a slight variation of the cyclic motif of the first movement:

EXAMPLE 20

A return to the first subject develops chiefly along rhythmic lines, perhaps beyond proper degree, before the reappearance of the lied melody warmly presented by the viola in A flat:

His Works: Chamber Music

EXAMPLE 21

With the concurrence of both violin and 'cello, the intensity mounts to the higher tone of B flat. Thereafter, all themes reappear: the first is recapitulated with modifications in triple tempo, the second follows in the key of C and is altered then rhythmically to support an "ff" return of the opening theme by all the strings, a dynamic augmentation which culminates in the forceful intervention of the cyclic theme

EXAMPLE 22

used as if to restore order and the original A Major tonality. When the agitation has subsided, the serene lied melody again makes an appearance, this time as a breathing pause before a determined return to the movement's first subject and the Piano Quartet's opening theme, now resolving in majestic close.

The last of Chausson's works for chamber group, the String Quartet in C minor, Opus 35, was left incomplete by his death in 1899. The fine style manifest in this composition, and the sobriety and confidence exuded by it equal those of the Piano Quartet. In the first movement (*grave, puis modéré*), a very august introductory theme becomes, in various guises and forms, the subject for the whole movement:

EXAMPLE 23

His Works: Chamber Music

It is obvious that by now Chausson's musical development
has attained its highest point: after the long period in which
the composer's primary preoccupation was harmonic, the
trend now is definitely established along lines of pure melody
elaborated with his perfected harmonic concepts. The second
movement (*très calme*) bears witness to this, with the two
lovely songs that comprise it in A flat and A flat minor.
Nothing is simpler and more felicitously outlined than the
simple lied form of this movement. Much more complicated
in structure is the third movement (*gaíment et pas trop vite*),
more contemplative than effusive. After the first statement
of the theme in F minor, the second part follows immediately in E (pivoting on the A-flat/G-sharp tone):

EXAMPLE 24

There is a short development before this theme returns in the
dominant C minor, and then in the coda and final development in a new 5/8 rhythm. D'Indy, who finished the work,
reported that the composer never wrote beyond page forty-
eight of the printed score (the A. Durand et Fils edition).[7]
Based on a few but valuable indications left by Chausson, the
remaining four pages of the work, its finale written in C, is
his friend's. According to Chausson's plans, this movement
was to have been the scherzo; apparently he was planning to

[7] "Ernest Chausson," *Cobbett's Cyclopedic Survey of Chamber Music,*
I, 270.

write a last movement in which he would have returned to the key of F. Most interesting about the String Quartet is the high concentration of its melodic essence and its rich flavor which impregnates a sober harmonic tissue with an unusually deep poetic quality. The last long composition by Ernest Chausson presents a picture of intense coloring, yet without violent tints.

From a performer's point of view, Chausson's music for chamber groups suffers from the same difficulties already encountered in the accompaniments of the *Mélodies:* difficulties of chromatic complication, doubling of parts, and filling in with trills, tremolos, and arpeggios. Though we might wish at times that the composer had been more self-critical and circumspect about such facile devices, they are usually not overdone and are overshadowed by the ideas, which are fine in themselves and are given commensurate treatment.

It is surprising, in a way, that a composer who was so relaxed when working at shorter genres should have left us so few numbers for single or accompanied instrument. But, as every projected composition loomed as a challenge to him, pieces such as *Paysage, Quelques danses,* or the *Pièce* for violoncello were treated with as much earnestness as the Symphony or the Piano Quartet. And if his standards, however relative, were not met, the new work would be destroyed, as happened to the *Cinq fantaisies* for pianoforte, Opus 1. His integrity could not allow this first endeavor, with uncertain harmonies and a melodic ingenuousness that was punctuated by trite snatches of Meyerbeer and Johann Strauss, to remain listed among his opera. Opus 26, on the other hand, a Dédicace and Sarabande, a Pavane, and a Forlane for piano

grouped under the collective title of *Quelques danses,* deserves inclusion in most pianists' repertoires. Poignantly classical and impersonal at all times, it nevertheless succeeds rather
well in investing us with a quaint harmonic curiosity. Here
Chausson is every inch himself, his contained self. In 1903 we
read Debussy's testimony to this effect, to which he adds:
"One must love them all, these dances," especially the Sarabande.[8] True, Debussy's appreciation was enhanced by a
strong feeling of kinship for his recently deceased and bereaved friend. But his comment need not be dated: there is
more than sufficient musical virtue in the twenty pages of the
Quelques danses to justify his judgment. Three Debussyan
qualities are required for playing the Opus 26. The Sarabande must be performed with full awareness of tonal unity,
as the Pavane can only be effective if understood in its stream-
of-consciousness style, and the Forlane, with its rapid gait, if
the pianoforte were considered a hammerless instrument.
Here is another of the many instances in which Chausson
proves he needs no extramusical stimuli to prod his compositions: more than poetic or pictorial, these numbers are in-
trinsically musical.

The *Paysage* for piano, Opus 38, is equally impersonal. In
a way, it seems to apply Debussy's statement to the effect that
music is destined not to the more or less exact reproduction
of nature, but rather to the mysterious concordances which
exist between nature and the imagination. What was the
"landscape" remembered by Chausson? Perhaps the one seen
from Fiesole, for his music has all the serenity and relaxation
of the Tuscan Apennines.

[8] Vallas, *Les Idées de Claude Debussy,* 70–71.

Ernest Chausson

Opus 39 is the *Pièce* for violoncello (or viola) and piano, a true gem of its kind, unpretentious and unsparkling, yet commanding our interest, if only, knowing Chausson, for the confidence that rings from its notes, the same confidence present in the Piano Quartet. Its merit is in its *"beauté sensible,"* the immediate enjoyment it procures by insinuating itself within us without our making any effort to grasp it. At once stately and tasteful, the *Pièce* never loses its gradually accelerated feeling of flow until the last page, when a return of the opening phrase serves to terminate a singularly lovely musical concept.

From the *Poème de l'Amour et de la Mer,* the interlude, an entity in itself, was arranged for pianoforte. Beautiful as it is in its original setting, out of context it seems to lose much of its meaning. At best, it can be used as an encore number, or as a theme. With its haunting melody, it may be considered the most characteristic theme by which to evoke the memory of Ernest Chausson.

Orchestral Music and the *Poème*

IF Chausson has gained a secure repertory status outside France, it has been mainly through his concert favorite Symphony in B-flat Major and his recital favorite *Poème* for violin and orchestra. Another orchestral number, *Viviane,* a symphonic poem based on a legend of the Round Table, is seldom performed, and still another, *Soir de fête,* also for orchestra, exists only in manuscript form. Yet it is not without difficulty and certainly not with surprise that we discover, in these last two works, pages of considerable attraction to those interested in the French composer.

Although posterior to the Trio, *Viviane,* Opus 5, is a youthful composition, young in exuberance and accordingly a little wanting in discipline. Such is, for instance, the whole middle section, which could, perhaps, stand some development. But it is an effective number, relying heavily on the suggestiveness of instrumental effects, on an orchestration which is clear and unburdened despite a rather generous use of tremolos and trills. In this respect, the volatile harp scoring of the last thirteen pages describing Merlin's sleep, notes that disappear like so many beads unstringing, is of great attraction, as are the overtone passages in the strings which abet it, and the distant, off-stage sounds of trumpet calls. The opening fifteen measures too, consisting of slowly ambulating chromatic chords before the serene entrance of a French horn solo, are lovely mood setters (Chausson used these same chords in the second act of *Le Roi Arthus,* just before Merlin's appearance). This horn theme,

EXAMPLE 25

as it underlines the atmosphere of the whole work, is of engaging tranquillity, never losing its softness as it passes from one instrument or from one rhythmic modification to another. The atmosphere is quite characteristic of Chausson, the one for which he wrote most willingly: the enchantment of vaporous contours, the mysterious poetry of an artist for whom nature bore an intimate meaning. Accents of Wagner and Franck are audible, but more clearly we hear the Chausson of the coming *Poème de l'Amour et de la Mer, Dans la Forêt du Charme et de l'Enchantement,* and *Poème.*

A portion of the medieval legend of King Arthur describes an episode involving the enchanter Merlin and his mistress Vivian. As the story goes, Merlin, infatuated with her beauty, confides to her one of his magic spells, and the lady, not believing in this special charm, tries it out on him. The result is that the enchanter is irretrievably entrapped in a hawthorn bush. Chausson departed slightly from this version of the legend, having made use of an Amoritic version as told by

His Works: Orchestral

Villermarqué. The composer's own synopsis of the various scenes suggested by his tone poem reads as follows:

Vivian and Merlin in the Forest of Broceliande. Love scene.

Trumpet calls. King Arthur's messengers scour the forest in search of the enchanter.

Merlin remembers his errand; he wants to flee and escape from the arms of Vivian.

Enchantment scene. To detain him, Vivian puts Merlin to sleep and surrounds him with blossoming hawthorns.

A destroyed work, *Solitude dans les Bois,* Opus 10, seems to have been conceived in a similar tonal setting, although here the mood was to have been even vaguer and more suggestive, more purely musical than *Viviane*. Chausson thought of it as "a poem which I make up alone in my head and of which I only give a general impression to the public. . . . There is no description in it, no hint of a story; only feelings."

Quite a surprise, indeed, one receives when one hears the symphonic poem *Soir de fête,* Opus 32, written in San Domenico di Fiesole in 1898. The first part, in particular, is quite different from anything Chausson ever wrote, a fact which is related undoubtedly to the very subjective impressions he tried to translate, the misunderstanding of which was responsible for the public's cold reactions to the work. In a letter to Octave Maus in October, 1898, Chausson, denying he ever intended to depict a true feast of any kind, offered the following explanation: "I simply wanted to note down a personal impression of the distant noise of a crowd; as contrast, the calm and serene night. The difficulty lay in the transposition. To give the idea of a joyful throng without employing any of those rhythms and phrases which seem to be obligatory in characterizing a celebration. . . . I realize that if one has the preconceived idea of a realistic 'fair,' *Soir de fête* must appear to be a kind of wager on an obscure and incomprehensible subject." Hence, any justification of the work must be made in recognition of Chausson's poetic intention: the movement of a gay and turbulent crowd in the soft silence of night, a feast which is not localized and is exteriorized into the absolute vague of a dreamer's mind.

Among the chief merits of the composition is its mature, relatively simple, and limpid orchestration. At no time is its style marred by vulgar effects. Movement is rendered more by numerous and fleeting modulations than by bouncing rhythmic patterns. Perhaps, in the long run, the constant shifting from one tonality to another becomes a little tedious to the ear, like a harmony student's involved experiment, but it serves the purpose of suggestion and of precluding the possibility of plastic description. Although *Soir de fête* does not lend itself to thematic analysis, we might select various subjects. The opening one, stated by the violoncellos,

EXAMPLE 26

is intense with life and is followed by a fast-moving development in triplet form. An even faster theme for clarinet solo

EXAMPLE 27

is developed mostly by woodwinds and strings over a press-
ing but even  rhythm, and stopped when the
strings introduce another phrase:

EXAMPLE 28

A melodic calm from clarinet and oboe emerges from
under the strings, and, allowing a few mysterious notes from
the French horns to drift past, establishes the calmer mood
of evening:

Oboe

EXAMPLE 29

After being crossed by the dying bursts of the now distant
festivity, this very calm section in 9/8 time, grazed by the
fleeting harmonies of harp runs and stilled by a few measures

Ernest Chausson

of violin solo, is extended, suggesting the vague rustle of nature's slumber. We recognize the familiar discreet and dreamy sensitivity of the composer of *Viviane,* the Concert, and the Symphony. The brusque change in setting from light to shade is accomplished simply by modulating from the joyous themes in A flat Major to the restful phrases in E Major. Then, the return of the A flat key signifies the return of light and festivity in all its sparkle, with the trumpets reintroducing the first subject, horn and clarinet soli developing the third from 3/4 to 3/8 time before an eventual doubling of the tempo, the oboe piercing through to carry the theme in turn, encouraged by a rollicksome tambourine and later by the other woodwinds and the strings. This pattern of whirling movement, passing at one point from a 12/8 to a 3/4 time and not devoid of a certain monotony due to a kind of back and forth parading of instruments, continues until a precipitous *"rapide"* section swells the orchestra into a resounding "fff." But the E Major key re-enters, and again we are introduced into the quiet nocturnal world of brushing harmonies, this time additionally softened by muted strings and harp flurries into a "ppp." Far from being confusing, the alternation between the two tonalities and, consequently, between the two settings, intensifies the double nature of Chausson's inspiration and the interest of his poetic design. If not his most successful work, *Soir de fête* remains perhaps his most original.

THIS IS what an ardent admirer of Ernest Chausson, Mr. K. S. Sorabji, says about the Symphony in B flat: "In this great work Chausson shows a mastery as consummate and as complete in the spacious form of the symphony as he does in the song, and at the same time as personal and as individual. . . . The Symphony is a work at once of richness, splendour and nobility of style, an elevated beauty of expression and thought. Chausson has no need to plaster his lofty exalted thought with a 'nobilmente' signboard. . . . The elevated plane of his musical thinking speaks for itself, with a natural, an inherent and unforced eloquence, lovely, rare and inexpressibly moving. Not the least of the artistic triumphs accomplished in this great work is the diversity of mood and expression—a diversity that in lesser men would make for confusion and scrappiness—but which, such is the organizing power of a great master such as Chausson, only reflects more light upon the magnificent grasp and control of the whole—a superbly unified diversity."[1]

Indeed, the Symphony's sober architecture, the composer's "unforced" mastery of his material, and his orchestration which points to an author from whom the art holds no secrets, in no way reveal the hours of inspirational anguish undergone by Chausson in the throes of penning this most popular work of his, this "scoundrel," as he termed it. The composition is cast in a cyclic mold. In this context, the term "cyclic," invented by D'Indy, implies a structural ideal: the achievement of unity in the complex variety of the large musical forms through the repetition and/or transformation of material across the several movements of a symphony, sonata, or quartet. Though not as rigorously cyclic as Franck's Symphony which is built around six notes introduced in the first movement, Chausson's work approaches the same idea in that

[1] *Mi Contra Fa*, 121 f.

165

it begins and ends with the same theme, suggests in the second movement the principal theme of the third, and uses the main subject of the first movement during the course of the finale. Hence the guiding thought is never lost. If extraneous materials also enter the mold, they are fused into the greater whole like strengthening metals in an alloy, serving at once to consolidate the musical structure and to bring out more clearly its character. The extreme variety of aspects, impressions, and colors, clustered, as it were, around a single theme, results in a highly successful and appealing work of "unified diversity."

Clarinet, horn, and lower strings begin the introductory section of the first movement (*lent,* B flat Major, 4/4 time) with a clearly defined, broad, and severe figure:

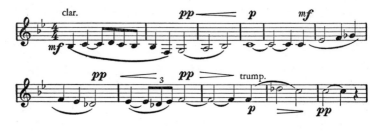

EXAMPLE 30

The mood is established. This is the theme that reappears forcefully in the finale. By the end of the sixth page of delicate counterpoint it is brought to a quick climax, just before the chief motive of the movement's main body (*allegro vivo,* B flat, 3/4), stated by horn and bassoon. It is healthy, but its joy is restrained:

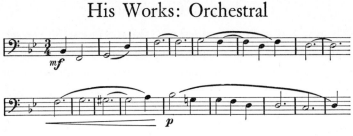

EXAMPLE 31

This is in turn counterstated by the oboe and worked into another climax. An upward and downward staccato figure by the woodwinds in B flat minor pentatonic, more exuberant in its joy than the previous theme,

EXAMPLE 32

serves as transition to the second theme, given out by clarinet, violas, and 'cellos, beginning in F sharp Major and tenderly melancholic in quality:

EXAMPLE 33

167

Ernest Chausson

The third idea which constitutes this second section of the first movement follows immediately, played by the violins:

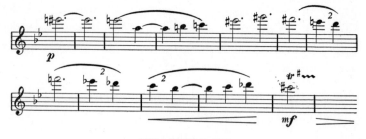

EXAMPLE 34

These ideas are briefly and simultaneously considered until the opening of the development section (*allegro scherzando*) in F sharp minor, relying heavily on the principal subject of the movement. The three ideas of the second section are also elaborately developed now through key changes and contrasting moods. The theme of the introduction is heard, too, and the development ends with rising violin and woodwind scales, capped by a diminuendo run of the clarinets in thirds which leads into the recapitulation. In this section (*allegro vivo,* B flat), the horn and harp present a slightly altered main subject:

EXAMPLE 35

effectively supported by violins and flutes, but only to give way shortly afterward to the same theme in its original form, quoted three octaves higher by the violins. The second and third ideas of the second section comprise the remainder of the recapitulation, appearing in flute and English horn in G Major and in the violins in D Major respectively. Then the principal and second themes are heard simultaneously in the original key before a short coda (*presto,* 4/4), built around the former theme which has here become binary.

The second movement (*très lent,* D minor, 4/4) emerges solemnly with a passage for strings, clarinet, bassoon, and two horns, marked "with a great intensity of expression." It is at first a deep and smothered lamentation, beginning and ending in D minor, without far-straying modulations:

EXAMPLE 36

This is fully exposed, and is followed by a haunting phrase serving as a contrasting idea in the same key and given out

first by the English horn, then by the clarinet, against soft
pulsations in the lower strings:

EXAMPLE 37

The two themes return together, before the movement's middle section (*un peu plus vite*) in B flat Major which is introduced by the English horn and solo 'cello in unison under a
broken chord accompaniment by violins and violas:

EXAMPLE 38

This expressive discourse is in time taken up by the violins (*doux et très chanté*) under woodwind ornaments. Though embellished with a delicate figuration, the melody remains sad and inconsolable. During the course of a considerable and striking climax, the brasswinds assume dominating importance and, together with the strings, clearly foreshadow the principal subject of the coming third and final movement, while a highly varied restatement of the slightly altered main subject of the first movement concludes the present movement in D Major.

In the final movement, an introductory passage (*animé,* B flat Major, 4/4, beaten 2/2) finds the winds crisply and loudly suggesting the principal theme, which is to be delivered by 'cellos and basses at the twenty-ninth measure, marked *"très animé"*:

EXAMPLE 39

The curiously colored background of the movement is due to sustained horn chords. Counterstatements by violins in the upper octaves over pulsing woodwind figures gradually make way for a brief transition which, by an interesting contrapuntal device, leads to a thunderous chromatic scale in unison. This, in turn, introduces the second subject of the movement in the style of a broad, serene chorale announced by the full orchestra in D Major (*encore plus animé*) and extended by the oboe before being recalled by the violins:

EXAMPLE 40

A very fleet, staccato variation of the first movement's principal theme in B flat Major (*très animé*) marks the beginning of the development section:

EXAMPLE 41

This is led through several swift modulations, until the chorale theme tops a climax and proceeds to dominate the rest of the development as it appears lyrically in one solo instrument, then another. With little warning, a sudden crescendo re-introduces the movement's principal subject with full orchestra. An extensive transition makes up for a lack of counter-statements, and the second theme, returning quietly with the solo horn in D Major (*un peu plus lent*), seems completely prepared. Now strings and woodwinds waste no time in returning the melody "fortissimo" before leading the whole orchestra into a new sequel. Woodwinds and violas, then horn, then strings, continue the phrase before a grandiose coda is intoned (*grave, 4/4*). This concluding section capitalizes on the introduction to the first movement, played by the brasswinds, picked up by the violins during vague references made to the main theme of the finale, and stated for a last time by bassoon, horn, and lower strings in the final four bars of the softly ending symphony.

Of all Chausson's endeavors, the Symphony lends itself most readily, perhaps, to criticism. Its abundance, marvelously corroborated by a rich, sonorous orchestration, may be considered to lack the concentration and sober power of the Piano Quartet or the *Chanson perpétuelle,* or, if profound lyricism be our criterion, the human strains of the *Poème.* But relative considerations cannot dispel our awareness of the breath of genius which pervades the whole work. Many times it has been said, also, that the Symphony is the work of an author impregnated beyond originality with the influence of his adored teacher César Franck. To be sure, the Flemish master left his imprint on Chausson as he did on other contemporaries, despite Debussy's statement: "César Franck's influence on French composers boils down to very little: he taught them certain writing methods, but their inspiration has no relation to his."[2] It is true, however, that due

2 Quoted from Léon Vallas, *Les Idées de Claude Debussy,* 69.

to his natural gifts of elegance and clarity, Chausson "frees himself and walks along his own path."[3] Though relying on Franck's Symphony for examples of framework and construction (including the chorale section), there is not the heavy churchlike contemplation, the sense of divine ecstasy that links the Belgian composer with Bach and Buxtehude. While not denying Franck's excellence, we can say that Chausson's emotion is more grateful, less complicated, and with fresher impulses. This is because it is essentially more monodic and less polyphonic than his master's. Moreover, there are fewer chromatic meanderings, and his eloquence is not marred by occasional "pull-stop" tendencies of improvisation or "filling-out" developments. Unencumbered by theories and problems and with far greater rhythmical variation, his music seems to speak more freely. The strongest criticism leveled against the cyclic form is that it tends to monotony and inevitability; but whereas the working out of themes under such conditions may be obvious in Franck's work, it is much less so in his pupil's. To his teacher, Chausson owed the maxims which governed his artist's life and his private concepts of music (concepts like the avoidance of technical skill or the superiority of pure music), not the particular ingredients of style. The signs of Chausson's individuality, therefore, are not merely suggestive, as one might expect from such a full-fledged member of the Franckist school, but, to an appreciable extent, positive, especially if considered from the point of view of stylistic and personal synthesis. The style of the Symphony is his own, inasmuch as it appears to be dictated by a highly intimate mood.

[3] *Ibid.*

His Works: Orchestral

For the Symphony in B flat is Chausson in his most characteristic guise of elegiac and dramatic attitudes intensified by a tragic sentiment. If we allow ourselves for a moment to be carried along somewhat questionable, yet possible, paths of fancy, we may find it interesting to consider the work as being dictated subconsciously by his biography. What is more intimate in its speculation than the double suggestion of the Symphony, once we have viewed the life of the composer of *Le Roi Arthus:* the sad restlessness in search of an ideal and the majesty of mysticism?

The opening of the Symphony indicates a mood of searching meditation which is then pierced by an idea of hope, a dream pleading for realization. At one point, there is even a feeling of self-domination awaiting new developments. These seem to come by means of short melodic phrases, sinuously linked with ordered continuity and expressing, at times also happily, the further hopes of a man who thinks he has overcome a first range of obstacles. But after this contained enthusiasm, the second movement appears to provide a measure of illusion, made poignant by the bitterness of doubt. The title should be "Grief." Slow movements best betray the inner temperament of a composer's soul. Majesty here has a kind of tragic grandeur. In no way does it imply weariness, but rather a sense of irreparableness still distant from desolation. Hence the third movement's imposing opening phrase cannot invoke revolt. If the man corrects himself and continues his restless struggle in quest of his ideal, he must do so now with less confidence than at first. His inquietude is submitted to ever increasing peripeteia until it finds rest in a religious truth announced by the prayer-like chorale. The soul may be resigned to suffering, but it remains aware of its dignity.

One might also find in this Symphony, psychologically interpreted, certain parallels with Chausson's generation, guided, of course, by his personal appeal to confidence and mysticism. When, then, to these qualities we add the realities of sorrow and submission, some of us may feel we have listened to a work of truly Christian inspiration. But others may feel—and very understandably—that it is misleading to attribute such heavy concepts of religious mysticism to a composer who had no running discourses with God or even pervading concern with the hereafter in the same manner as César Franck. Nothing prevents us, however, from accepting the suggested mysticism in a purely metaphysical and artistic sense, the way we interpret the Ideal sought by the Arthur-Chausson of *Le Roi Arthus*. With this acceptance we should be closer to the composer, as an artist and thinker.

THE POET's thoughts which search night and calm away from the festival in *Soir de fête,* the slowly absorbing enchantment of *Viviane,* and the melancholic dignity that marks the Symphony, seem to combine their murmurs in the *Poème* for violin and orchestra, Opus 25. It epitomizes Chausson's style, adding to it a strong measure of vitality, a quality lacking in the *Mélodies.* The musical idea expands, assumes greater solidity and breadth, along with more simplicity. Essentially melodic, its curves are firm, beautiful, and finely inflected. It would be difficult to find, in the composer's literature, a phrase more generous and elevated than the ruling

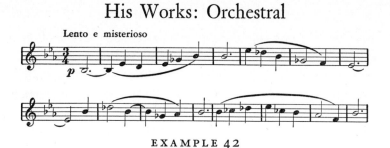

EXAMPLE 42

or the noble, movingly sorrowful

EXAMPLE 43

In the *Poème,* Chausson abandons many of his inhibitions and proclaims his lyricism frankly. Yet it is contained, in some respects, because, though deeply sentimental, it stops short of that sentimentality which offends the canons of taste by nourishing exaggeration and sensationalism. Its emotional sensuousness is due more to his exploitation of all the technical and expressive powers of the violin than to any want of refinement in inspiration. "It is tender and twilit, and its entrancement is not due to whine or maudlin sentiment," Sorabji would say.[4] Richly inventive and often unexpected, his harmonies succeed one another logically and never offensively to the ear. On the contrary, they caress it. This continuous, intertwining movement in the modulations ends by producing a web of sound which communicates very gratify-

[4] See 74n.

ingly both melancholy and meditation, the two attributes of a lyric "poem." What Pierre de Bréville wrote in his memorial article about Chausson in 1899 may be applied here: ". . . all his works exhale a dreamy sensitiveness. . . . His music is saying constantly the word *'cher.'* "[5]

On the one hand, the *Poème* is composed with aristocratic distinction of manner, at times ethereal, and, on the other, it is more genuinely human than any of his other compositions, certainly more broadly human than the ivory-tower aestheticism of his friend Debussy. These seeming opposites, while not contradictory, do face each other in the soul of this composition, and explain its popularity—the charm and the *"cher"* that bring it closer to us than the works of Debussy. And the latter, let us add, was far from discounting the *Poème*. In 1913 he praised the ethereal atmosphere of the work in the following terms: "The *Poème* for violin and orchestra contains his best qualities. The freedom of its form never hinders harmonious proportion. Nothing touches more with dreamy sweetness than the end of this *Poème,* where the music, leaving aside all description and anecdote, becomes the very feeling which inspired its emotion. These are very rare instances in the works of an artist."[6]

[5] *Mercure de France,* September, 1899.

[6] Claude Debussy, *"Notes sur les Concerts du Mois,"* S. I. M. (Société Internationale de Musique), Vol. IX, No. 1 (January 15, 1913), 50–51.

Photograph by Alinari (Florence)

Chausson in 1896
The last photograph taken of him.

Dramatic, Choral, and Incidental Music

OF unequal importance to the Chausson listener are those compositions which must be considered in a dramatic context. Outside of *Le Roi Arthus,* such are: *Hélène,* a lyrical drama in two acts, including the section called *Le Jugement de Pâris;* the five incidental numbers for Shakespeare's drama *The Tempest* (*La Tempête*); and the musical setting of Maurice Bouchor's three-act drama, *La Légende de Sainte Cécile.* Other attempts by the composer, like *Les Caprices de Marianne, Jeanne d'Arc,* and *Les Oiseaux,* are unavailable.[1] Finally, not dramatic as such and more strictly choral are *L'Arabe,* the *Chant nuptial,* Dante's *Ballata,* and the *Hymne védique.*

The best-known published excerpt from *Hélène* is written for women's chorus (first soprani, second soprani, and contralti), scored as the *Jugement,* on Leconte de Lisle's evocative verses. An early work—Opus 7—it bears the stamp

---

[1] *Les Caprices de Marianne,* for the play by the same name by Alfred de Musset. A rough draft of the second "Entr'acte," "*La Mort de Coelio,*" exists in the library of the Paris Conservatory. It is in A Major, intended for an average orchestra, and is rather somberly scored. *Jeanne d'Arc* was intended, apparently, to be no longer than a short lyrical scene. *Les Oiseaux* was to have provided musical accompaniment for Aristophanes' play *The Birds.*

Ernest Chausson

of Massenet's school, which is equally evident in what exists of the still earlier *Les Caprices de Marianne*. A very strong religious, perhaps we should say psalmlike, feeling flows under the inspiration, revealing itself regularly through the sequence

EXAMPLE 44

but unable to ramify this nuclear idea into any convincing development. There is a basic incompatibility, it seems, between the pagan but not spiritual tenor of the poem and the spiritual mood of the music. Besides, the spiritual mood itself achieves its effect not through a sense of humility and tender understanding, which are qualities essential to religious expression, but rather through the exuberance of the composer's youth: it is the same untempered enthusiasm that reigned in his previous orchestral composition *Viviane* and that settled later with such fine composure in the Concert, the *Poème,* and much of *Arthus*. The harmonies are conventional, the modulations often expected, the texture of the accompaniment dramatic, and the vertical writing simple. Together, these make for easy listening but fall short of being inspirational. The initial mistake had been made in selecting a text whose ample phraseology did not lend itself too well to musical commentary. Nonetheless, for us *Hélène* is an interesting effort on Chausson's part; it discloses at once those elements of his sensitivity—the lyrical and the religious—which he found cause to contain later, and which, let us add, in their new garb of containment, lost none of their fundamental emotivity and spirituality.

Less successful is *Le Jugement de Pâris*. It presents, to be sure, a well-wrought tempo development, advancing from a *"très calme"* to a *"plus vite"* to an *"encore plus vite"* and thence to an *"animé"* before settling in the final *"modéré."* Yet it does not differ appreciably in conception from *Hélène:* it retains the same simplicity and conventionality for modern ears, while appearing a little more belabored. Despite a full accompaniment, there is not sufficient elevation in tone and too little preoccupation with harmonic texture to give the work real stature in the choral repertory. Both *Hélène* and the *Jugement* are luxuriantly orchestrated. Because the latter orchestration was lost among the composer's papers and was not recovered until the death of his son Laurent in 1952, another was made by Louis Aubert in 1949. Although adequate, the original is still smoother in coloration.

To the choral repertory belong four numbers which have no dramatic intent other than that which is inherent in the text itself. The first of these—and the least polished—is the unpublished *L'Arabe,* for solo tenor with male chorus and orchestra. Its tempo development decreases from a *"très vite"* to a *"moins vite"* several times before the ending recapitulation. An insistent woodwind rhythm in 3/4 time gives pleasing movement to the text:

> *Vole, ami, vole, et tends les ailes,*
> *Comme un trait dévore l'espace . . . .*
> *. . . et sur les sables des déserts*
> *Ne laisse même une trace,*

Ernest Chausson

and an unusual effect arises from a tenor-viola/violas combination, but in general, the unrelieved recitative character of the solo voice does not make for too much interest.

On the text of Leconte de Lisle's poem, Chausson composed the *Chant nuptial,* Opus 15, for first and second soprani and first and second alti. More than a song, it is an elegy to marriage, the "divine brother of Eros." The poet, to use de Lisle's own words, has created ideas with "invisible or visible forms, living or conceived images." And the underlining music fits the poetic feeling respectfully, with taste, yet without attempting to follow the letter of the text. As a matter of fact, when the poem shifts from a description of the rite to the festive laughter of the guests, the score does nothing more than change from the original *"andante con moto"* to *"un peu plus vite"* without any alteration in the character of the music itself. This gives the *Chant nuptial* an easy, flowing quality and a measure of serenity which finds final utterance in the almost religious conclusion on the word "Hymen."

Opus 29, the *Ballata* from Dante Alighieri (*"In abito di saggia messaggera, Muovi, ballata...."*), was scored by Chausson for four voices *a cappella* (*sans lenteur,* 4/4, C Major). Its great attraction is a certain modality which gives genuine flavor to the verses of the thirteenth-century Italian poet. The polyphonic horizontal writing is clear, the enharmonic movement moderately effective, but the ending, with a slow climb to the fifth of the tonic tone, sounds too conventional for the medieval frame of reference in which we view the poem and in which the music itself has placed us at the outstart. Perhaps a need for revision accounts for the fact that the *Ballata* has not been published.

His Works: Incidental

The *Hymne védique,* Opus 9, dedicated to César Franck, is much more impressive and even more dramatic than the previously mentioned dramatic works. Leconte de Lisle again supplies the poetic inspiration. This time we are concerned with a full, mixed chorus, whose individual voices are frequently separated. The unaccompanied entrance of the tenors and basses (at the eleventh measure in a harmonic pattern that repeats itself several times later with greater intensity) has a sacerdotal quality of marked awe. The "Vedic" verses of the poet of the *Poèmes barbares* are very adequately colored by Chausson's orchestration which makes especially effective use of the lower-range instruments. However abstruse the poem due to the listener's unfamiliarity with Hindu religious beliefs, the music's many climaxes, its driving power, and its sober but primitive declamatory force (which, at one point, swells an already "ff" chorus into an even more strident "fff") acts as an unmistakable commentary. The dramatic puissance and its ascendancy make us feel we have discovered a new Chausson when we hear the *Hymne védique.*

Gracious indeed, by contrast, is the incidental music, Opus 18, written for Shakespeare's *Tempest.* It is in five parts, three for voice (or voices) with orchestral background and two for orchestra. The first, *Chant d'Ariel,* has all the lightness and airiness necessary for the tricksy spirit. Although the music does make a conscious attempt to explain Bouchor's translation down to the volatile quality of "quivering breeze" and the actual barking of a dog (an endeavor which usually destroys unity), this number can be extracted from its collection and sung as a humorous counterpart to any *Mélodie.* The second part is a fast (*allegro vivo*) orchestral section called *Air de danse*. It, too, is sporting and dainty, losing none of its rapid gait from beginning to end and exhausting its snappy energy in a final "pianissimo" chord in the upper register. The orchestration is never overcharged. Third is a "Duet between Juno and Ceres." It is calmer, with the voices (at first individually introduced, then combined) engaged in a curiously liturgic-like melody over a rolling accompaniment. A few well-chosen modulations give its detached character sufficient movement. At the opening of the fourth section, *Danse rustique,* there is a long bucolic piper's tune, scored for the flute. It leads into a very fresh country dance of lively, engaging delicacy, beginning in moderate cut-time and increasing both in tempo and dynamics until it is brought to a sparkling finish. The final section is the *Chanson d'Ariel,* again for single voice. A short allegretto, it does not have the frolic or mirth of the first number. The melodic line, over sustained background, accompanies the tired yet gracious meaning of the verses:

> *Quand je serai las de ma course folle et de ma chanson,*
> *J'irai me suspendre aux fleurs du buisson.*

Why *La Légende de Sainte Cécile,* Opus 22, should have received such iniquitous criticisms after its first performance is a little difficult to understand. Perhaps our ears today are better able to accept the dissonances and chromaticism of the three-act drama than those of 1892. Or perhaps sensitive purists were outraged at such a lighthearted, almost unmeditated, way of treating the patroness of music, St. Cecilia. Certainly, no one could have mistaken it for a serious religious drama, especially when it was written for Le Petit Théâtre des Marionettes!

Of all Chausson's works, the *Légende* is the most spontaneous and caused him the least trouble in writing. Beauty here is achieved through extreme simplicity. When the composer wishes dramatic effects, his music waxes chromatic; when he strives for continuity in sequences, it moves in diminished chords, ninths and sevenths. Simplicity engenders tenderness, while sudden yet smooth modulations establish drama. That is all. Hence the unity in music and conception that make the work a little masterpiece.

A breakdown is as follows:

Act I. 1) *"Entrée de Cécile—Mélodrame,"* a lovely section of romantic inspiration; 2) *"Mélodrame et choeur d'anges,"* rather religious and elevated; 3) *"Hymne liturgique de Saint Michel,"* a short, militant, and solemn page; 4) *"Mélodrame,"* a very condensed score with many modulations and the voices liturgical and spread; 5) *"Mélodrame,"* containing suave reminiscences of the previous section and the end of the first; 6) *"Choeur d'anges— Mélodrame,"* a long, moving, and elevated portion ending the first act.

Act II. 7) *"Cantique de Cécile"* with its 'cello solo, a page of true inspiration, lofty and religious beauty, possibly the most moving in the whole drama; 8) *"Musique de scène—Entrée de Cécile,"* a reminiscence of the first subject, short and not too significant; 9) *"Musique de scène—Sortie de Cécile et de Valérien,"* a section of lighter and pleasing simplicity, concluding the second act.

Act III. 10) *"Prélude et choeur d'anges,"* dramatic, yet beautifully restrained, almost operatic in quality; 11) *"Choeur d'anges,"*

Ernest Chausson

a sweet and simple passage; 12) *"Mélodrame et choeur d'anges,"* a dramatic section relying heavily on chromatic effects; 13) *"Mélodrame, choeur et musique de scène—Mort du roi,"* a tender and light scene with an exceptionally fine ending in the high register; 14) *"Musique de scène—Sortie de Cécile,"* again the first theme in short, gracious, and transitional manner; 15) *"Scène finale—Apparition de Sainte Cécile,"* the long, melodious, simple, and yet full ending of the drama accompanied by harp enlacements to enhance its ethereal quality.

It would be hard to surpass in spontaneity the exquisite charm of *La Légende de Sainte Cécile,* a charm which is nourished slowly as the miniature drama unfolds its naïve, unostentatious garb. Section seven especially, is worthy of high recognition. Its captivating 'cello theme

EXAMPLE 45

and the vocal melody built around it, as we have indicated previously, can be ranked among the best pages of religious music Chausson ever penned.

The Opera

IN his palace in Carduel and surrounded by all his friends and knights, King Arthur celebrates his victory over the Saxon invaders. Only his sage counselor Merlin is not present. During the celebration, the King praises all his warriors, but above all he lavishes fine words on the valiant and loyal Lancelot. In this he is accompanied by a chorus of bards. Jealous knights, however, murmur concealed dissatisfaction and are abetted by Mordred, who by chance has overheard the King's spouse, the lovely Guinevere, remind Lancelot of a tryst that night (Act I, scene 1).

On the appointed night, Lancelot's faithful squire Lionel is on a terrace of the royal castle and in a state of great concern: his master is betraying the King. He can only hope that Mordred will not discover him. Guinevere and Lancelot come forth, aware only of their mutual love which their impassioned words are constantly reaffirming. Lionel warns them of daybreak, but before the lovers can separate Mordred arrives shouting treason. Angrily, Lancelot pierces him with his sword and Mordred falls. Lancelot then asks Guinevere to join him in a neighboring forest. Before she leaves, however, she has time to see Mordred, whom she thought dead, get up, aided by his soldiers (Act I, scene 2).

Ernest Chausson

At the edge of a pine forest, Lancelot awaits his mistress. He is rather anxious: what if Mordred were not dead? The thought induces a feeling of remorse for having deceived his King. All is brought to a climax when Guinevere arrives in fright, asking her lover to save her, for Mordred who is alive has proceeded to turn all the knights against him. Only one man defends him believing him innocent: King Arthur himself. He wants his favorite knight to return to Carduel to swear he is not guilty, and if he does, he, Arthur, will believe him. Now Lancelot is in the throes of a drastic psychological situation, torn between love and duty. Knowing he cannot lie, the Queen, almost in panic, tries to turn his attention to her lost honor and his cowardice if he abandons her. Her pleas and cries are apparently in vain, until she actually chases him away. Then Lancelot reluctantly feels he must lie and later seek death in combat. Guinevere, however, would prefer to flee with him, thereby renouncing her royalty in favor of a lifetime together. The prospect of complete liberty in a distant land is enticing, and Lancelot yields to this selfish solution (Act II, scene 1).

In his palace Arthur is waiting for Lancelot to return, still unwilling to believe in his guilt. Nonetheless, by now he cannot hinder some doubt from emerging, for, despite the Saxons' defeat, he knows that the institution of the Round Table, to whose creation and organization he has devoted all his energies and ideals, is being ruined by the private passions of his knights. He is well aware of Mordred's jealousy and of his desire to dethrone him. Discouraged, therefore, he invokes his old friend and enchanter Merlin, who now appears to him with a long white beard, through the foliage of a tree. The spirit's prophecy is not hopeful: "Let Arthur hope for nothing in the future; the Round Table will perish." Both Arthur and Merlin had counted too much on man's virtue; even the enchanter's prophecies had been betrayed by this trust. So now he prefers to withdraw to his secret prison. Arthur will die, concludes the spirit, but only until the day of his glorious awakening. These somber words leave the King unmoved; his only interest is in the more immediate present, namely, Guinevere is innocent, is she not? and Lancelot too? Merlin does not answer. He vanishes. To his unspeakable grief, Arthur understands. He screams for his knights, and all gather as the news is reported that the Queen has disappeared with Lancelot. Confusion now reigns: some knights want to take this opportunity to abolish the Round Table; others, siding with the King, wish only to silence the traitors. All leave crying death to the abductor (Act II, scene 2).

On the crest of a hill dominating the battlefield, Guinevere watches the battle below as it is being described to her by an old squire, Allan. In the meantime, Mordred, left alone in Carduel, has proclaimed himself king. The formerly valiant and intrepid Lancelot now appears, having fled the field of battle. Following Guinevere's desire, he had fought, but having seen Arthur, brandishing his heroic sword Excalibur, he had not had the courage to continue. In vain the lady insists; Lancelot, reassuming mastery of his honor, has decided to give himself up to Arthur. This time nothing can detain him. Guinevere's supplications are to no avail as the knight entrusts her to his squires and leaves. Sensing doom, the abandoned Queen sends the squires on a mission, then unfolds her long locks of "somber blue" hair with which she strangles herself (Act III, scene 1).

The battlefield by the sea is littered with soldiers. One of them, wounded ten times but still breathing, is Lancelot. "Arthur, I am here! I surrender to you! Take my sword! strike me down!" The King is without wrath: Lancelot has not dishonored him because Arthur's honor depended on himself alone. Yet he feels discouraged, now in the twilight of his life, having believed so confidently in effort, will, and ideal. But Lancelot's dying words provide a prophecy: he, in shame, dies forever, but Arthur's thought is immortal. "The love which elated your heart sprang from eternal fire. You shall live! You shall live!" Arthur forgivingly asks God to give his knight rest and sleep. Now an invisible chorus sings of a pure hero and of a great, wounded soul which the angels are inviting to escape beyond the stars to that mysterious world where secrets are unveiled. A boat of maidens, one winged, floats towards the shore, coming over the sea from a gilded horizon beyond which the sun is setting. Arthur says farewell to all that he loves: his country, his adventures, and his sword. Then he disappears behind a cliff, and the boat is seen later bearing him as if asleep into the golden-purple sunset, as the chorus chimes a celebration of him who had the supreme glory of believing in the Ideal (Act III, scene 2).

Such are the story elements chosen by Chausson for his interpretation of a twelfth-century legend pertaining to the "Cycle of the Round Table" which he called *Le Roi Arthus,* Opus 23. His penchant for the vocal expressiveness of music, joined to a great feeling for orchestral sonority, was to lead him naturally to one of the highest forms of expression for the theater: lyrical drama.

Through lyrical drama, Chausson conveys to us symbolically his faith in a most precious ideal. He saw in the Round Table's strong society an island of civilization in a sea of barbarism, one might say a replica of a most profound experience in his life: his membership in the Franck group. To his mind, the Knights of the Round Table and the Franckists shared a common ideal: the effort to better man, the former through justice and a social code, the latter through Art. Let us recall that in answer to a searching question—what is a man of good will to do in modern times?—he wrote: "Action is needed. . . . A work of art, too, is an action, perhaps the most significant which a man can accomplish."[1] The foregoing comparison does not imply that Arthur, the energetic statesman and warrior, is to be likened to César Franck, at least not specifically. Arthur is rather Chausson's concept of a great man, one who carries his own burden ("My honor! Do you think that it depends on any one but myself?"), and who, although fully aware of the imperfections around him, never weakens in his quest for a worthy ideal. A letter to Poujaud throws an interesting light on this thought:

You will not be surprised if I tell you that I do not at all share your opinion about "relaxed morality." I understand only effort, constant effort in all things, and always directed towards the same goal. What do you see that is not an effort? Even for the instinctive

[1] Letter to Bonheur, November 14, 1892.

artist, at least in our modern times, a work of art does not come about without will power. I regret it, as you, but I believe that it is necessarily so. We are no longer in the times when myths, and later, national legends, are formed by themselves.[2]

Similarly, in the opera, Arthur, seeing Lancelot expire and with him the dream of a perfect society, exclaims: "I believed in the power of effort, in the energy of will power,/ Without respite I have fought./ And now, what remains of all my life?/ Disappointed hopes—useless, useless efforts." It is here that Lancelot pronounces the immortality of the King's thought and dies proclaiming "You will live! You will live!" Because the King's ideal is that of the Franckist group and specifically of Chausson, for us the struggling Arthur becomes none other than Chausson himself. And his mystic death is less a measure of selfish hope than it is a counsel of idealistic perseverance, be it expressed in regards to the Franck school or more universally as an example to a gasping humanity, locked in eternal combat with materialistic, pragmatic, or existentialist forces.

WHILE THERE is an undeniable similarity between *Le Roi Arthus* and Wagner's *Tristan und Isolde* as subjects, and notwithstanding Chausson's own moaning about his treatment (the "red specter of Wagner that does not let me go" and the "frightful Wagner [who] blocks all my paths"), any comparison between the two composers which means to go beyond the external analogy of the same legendary cycle is both useless and dangerous. Chausson's Wagnerism is very limited

[2] August, 1888.

indeed; he was one of the rare composers of his time to be nearly immune to it. A few bars at the opening of the Symphony that recall the *Tetralogy,* a few Wagnerian whispers in *Viviane,* and the drama's conforming to some of the poetic rules of Bayreuth are all the factors we can single out for purposes of parallelism. Yet the opera, due to these rules and to the corresponding Lancelot-Tristan, Guinevere-Isolde, Arthur-Mark similarity, has been branded Wagnerian time and again.

Before attempting to vindicate his position vis-à-vis Bayreuth, we might quote at length an article by Chausson himself in the *Mercure de France* of April, 1897, in which he rallies to the defense of Vincent d'Indy, whose opera *Fervaal* had been labeled Wagnerian. Obviously aware of the analogies that could and would be drawn between *Arthus* and *Tristan,* he was forestalling hereby objections to his own opera and, by extension, justifying his music as a whole when he wrote:

Richard Wagner . . . , in upsetting the old and then frail structure of the opera by creating a new art form, greatly modified the dramatic conventions of his time. By virtue of genius and obstinacy, he finally triumphed, but the struggle is continuing after his death and under disadvantageous conditions, since he is no longer here to defend his theory by means of masterpieces. The question can therefore be summed up like this: Did Wagner simply find the form best suited to the nature of his genius or was he an initiator, pointing out a new theatrical orientation to future generations?

For me there is no doubt about the answer. Wagner was a pathbreaker, one of those rare and very great men who discover

Ernest Chausson

a yet unknown land in the realm of thought; he showed a new road on which one can set out without being charged with plagiarism. . .

Personality, this mysterious thing, shows itself everywhere through sensitiveness, taking the word in its widest sense. Thanks to it, the same object or the same feeling can give rise to very different manifestations of art. Imagine the same landscape painted by Corot or by Monet, the same tragic story dramatized by Racine or by Victor Hugo. *The subject in itself is of little consequence.*

In spite of first-rate musical and dramatic qualities, . . . *Fervaal* remains a transitional work. It is not a manifestation of a new art. It could hardly be otherwise. When a genius as powerful, as dominating as Richard Wagner appears in the world, he gives off so much splendor that after him there follows a kind of darkness . . . Hence general uncertainty, gropings, attempts in all directions in order to try escaping from the crushing glory, which seems to obstruct every road . . . it was like that in literature after Victor Hugo. Those are troubled, painful but not unfertile times. The literary movement in France which followed romanticism is proof of that. Is it an exaggerated optimism that makes me believe that it will be the same in French music? Whatever may happen, the name of Vincent d'Indy is among those who will certainly survive.

Let us be just. It is not among composers alone that the obsession with Wagner is noticeable. Music critics are still more violently struck by it. And that did not begin today. In 1875, during the first performances of *Carmen*—which were not successful, as is known—Bizet actually suffered from this accusation of Wagnerism. Bizet and many others. Lalo, Franck, now so much admired, Saint-Saëns, Fauré, all Wagnerians. What must we conclude from this? for this tenacious accusation supposes at least a semblance of truth. That Wagnerism is most frequently a momentary malady, which is cured by itself. Certain ninth chords were used to surprise formerly; they were called "Wagnerian," for this

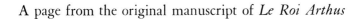

A page from the original manuscript of *Le Roi Arthus*

adjective is commonly used for everything which surprises. Since then they have become so familiar to us that we cannot understand how they could amaze us. They are no longer Wagnerian. I cannot help thinking that when time, this great judge, an almost infallible judge, will have passed judgment on *Fervaal,* the very real originality of D'Indy will appear with surprising clarity. Our sons will say to each other: "How was it possible that our fathers could not see the difference between this music and that of Wagner," and they will think they are better fortified than we. But, as it may perhaps be the fashion in those times, they will be accusing their contemporaries of imitating M. Salvayre.

Unavoidable, perhaps, was the encounter between Wagner and Chausson in the love scene, occuring on the terrace of the castle (Act I, scene 2). The same susurration and panting in the orchestra, its titillating timbers, quivering strings, and sighing woodwinds, reach the ear. But there is a good element of difference, which keeps the scene from falling into pastiches or flagrant reminiscences of the master from Bayreuth. It is in the atmospheres created: both are troubled, but where Wagner's is balsamic and incendiary, Chausson's is subtle and perfumed. It is also insidious; and here, as in many characteristics of his harmony, he is not looking back to the *Tetralogy* but ahead to *Pelléas et Mélisande.*

His simple, tender lyricism, melancholically stirred by what we have once called his aristocratic sensitivity, is quite different from the challenging or persuasive qualities of Wagnerian musical emotion. His melodies are broad and supple, tender and freely written, and have little in common with the planned thematic developments of the composer of *Tristan und Isolde.* Moreover, however sonorous, the orchestration of *Le Roi Arthus* is homogeneous and can hardly be said to emulate the whirling instrumental waves of the other. We might say, then, that despite the proximity of inspiration, Chausson was showing a new possible direction to the Wagnerian manner.

If now we analyze the German's and the Frenchman's character portrayals closely, we are immediately struck by the difference in the behavior of the knights after their sins. In the former's work, where King Mark is relegated to a secondary plane and the interest revolves around the two lovers, we witness the triumph and apotheosis of a fatal and inexorable erotic passion, whereas in the latter's, where Arthur takes the foreground, we are presented with an exaltation of duty, beauty, and moral grandeur. Next to him, Lancelot actually seeks death, after having torn himself away from Guinevere, because he recognizes the guilt of his love and can only hope to justify himself by expiation. This situation brings out the philosophy of the drama. Guinevere, in her criminal passion, and Lancelot, in his faithless weakness, are extinguished in a demise without honor. The egoistic satisfaction sought in their lives is destined to be eternally forgotten, whereas the noble social undertaking of the irreproachable Arthur will not perish throughout the ages.

From one point of view, the works of the two composers are curious. Wagner, a German, seems to have kept the Gaelic or Celtic background of the Round Table romances, in which love eclipses all other sentiments and even wins over the sacred ties of marriage. On the other hand, Chausson, a Frenchman, though finding material, like Wagner, in Geoffrey of Monmouth's *Historia Regum Britanniae* or its trans-

lation by Robert Wace called *Brut,* deals with an attitude
more resembling that of the primordial poems of the Germans and Franks—the "Chansons de Geste" of the Charlemagne cycle, *Beowulf,* the *Eddas*—in which moral attention
is directed toward a spouse's fidelity, a friend's loyalty, and a
paladin's respect for a faith sworn to his king. Lancelot, the
hero who will flee from the arms of his beloved, seek death
in order to cleanse his guilt and expire proclaiming Arthur's
nobility and prophesying his glory, turns out to resemble more
one of the Saxon thanes than the gallant, intrepid, yet sentimental and slightly frivolous knights of the Celts and Bretons.

The course of the forbidden love of the young protagonists
also differs in the two operas. In *Tristan und Isolde,* after a
night of intoxicated exaltation, the love grows even more
desperate and exasperated until death is welcomed as the only
possible relief from their voluptuous troubles. The point of
departure in *Le Roi Arthus* is the same, but after the first
ecstasies of consummated adultery, Lancelot grows remorse-
ful, feels himself more and more drawn to the side of his betrayed friend, and reassumes complete mastery of the rights
of his conscience and honor. His death is, therefore, redemp-
tional.

Not all the opera is melancholic or languorous, at least
not essentially, notwithstanding some opinions that have
been voiced to the contrary. To be sure, many are the pages
of the score that are characterized by the charm and abandonment typical of the composer, the poignant or resigned pathos
of sadness. But the tenor of the whole is masculine. The musical plot develops in accordance with the growth of the characters, and, in the long run, the veritable natures of both

Lancelot and Guinevere prevail. In the case of the former, it is his moral heroism which reacts against, and eventually dominates, his emotional weakness. A repentant Coriolanus, he is forgiven by his generous king. Likewise, Guinevere's stubbornness in her criminal love is energetic, a kind of flagitious grandeur approaching that of a Medea, Clytemnestra, or Lady Macbeth. She is a Frank indeed, as contemptuous of sacraments as the Frédégonde or Brunehaut of Merovingian times. There is never any doubt about Arthur's nature; as a symbol he cannot change. And he too was conceived Germanically, not as the Romanesque and thaumaturgical king of magic spells and devices and of wild, though brilliantly concluded, wagers of Chrétien de Troyes or of Wace's *Brut,* but rather the fundamentally pure and austere king, the "immaculate" monarch of Tennyson's *The Idylls of the King.* And, to conclude, certainly the lofty and majestic idealism that emerges at the end of the opera, a quality so unknown to the often naïve narrations of the Round Table, bears in its nobility a distinctive measure of power.

If we now leave Wagner aside and consider *Le Roi Arthus* alone, we note at once a highly meritorious feature: the scrupulous preservation of the natural inflections of speech in the sung language. Chausson, in writing his own libretto, has avoided all forms of pompousness which so often before his time had made for stylized recitatives or elaborate arias. Instead, the text often shines with unusual poetic qualities: *"Ta parole est sombre comme le rire de la mer"* (Arthur to Merlin, Act II, scene 2), for example, is a verse of rare beauty and fine imagery. *"Je n'ai plus rien d'humain que ma douleur"* (Arthur, Act III, scene 2) is likewise a verse of singular

His Works: The Opera

power, and sets off poetically the whole speech in which it appears. Moments such as these illuminate the otherwise adequate quality of the libretto and allow the composer to respect more fastidiously the gentle cadences of the French language. There is no concession to tradition in the form of hackneyed, trite material. On the contrary: as in the *Mélodies,* the words seem to want to eschew all showiness by merging into the accompanying symphony.

A second praiseworthy feature is the orchestral score of the opera, which is very polished and opulent without being overtaxed. Where passions are depicted, the music is tormented, and the lack of a precise tonality, due to running chromaticism and infinite modulations, might put a listener who has difficulty following an often vague melodic track in a state of inquietude. But there is much to make up for it: rich harmonies, smooth timber combinations, engaging themes and recitatives, and accurate accentuations of the libretto's unusual poetic qualities. The music explains both gestures and feelings. Moreover, the descriptive interludes and preludes and the choral ensembles, especially those of the denouement, are appealing in the way they effectively temper or heighten the moods.

The score opens with an alert, heroic prelude. A turbulent theme in C minor is followed by a more sustained martial motif, and this is followed in turn by a theme in E flat Major, the principal phrase proclaiming Arthur's glory and that of the society of the Round Table. At the climax the curtain rises. Arthur's opening peroration is underlined with joyous animation, counterbalanced later by the jealous sarcasms of the crafty Mordred. The song of the bards echoing Arthur is vigorous and rhythmical, and eventually gives way to a charming section in which Guinevere appears and sings: "Receive from my hands this vermilion cup." An orchestral transition constructed on the main themes of the prelude, but less heroic and more passionate, leads to the long ecstatic love scene which is accompanied by Lionel's vigilance and interrupted only by the combat between Mordred and Lancelot. The music captures convincingly the nocturnal atmosphere, punctured by Lionel's anxiety and Mordred's rage. On the whole, however, the first act is uneven, and the thematic formulas and harmonic sequences themselves, though not without value, are not as typical of Chausson as those we are to hear in the magnificent third act.

The second act begins with a calm, religious prelude. Its mood is carried by the recitative chant of a laborer sowing his fields. After this, Lancelot's monologue of remorse injects a dose of dramatic contrast: "My word lies, my happiness is marred." It is interesting to note with Pierre Lalo how Chausson seems more at ease in rendering certain feelings than others, how, for instance, this repentance of Lancelot rings truer and more expressive to our ears than the immediately following and equally agitated exhortations of Guinevere which sound somewhat arbitrary and uncertain and betray the composer's effort. Chausson's lyricism seemed embarrassed when called upon to express feelings that were too removed from the composer himself. Hence Lancelot's disloyalty and Guinevere's perverseness are musically less successful than Arthur's generosity and faith in his Ideal, Merlin's sadness, and Lancelot's contrition. The dialogue between the anxious king and the disaffected magician especially is one of the most effective sections of the opera. Following an interlude based on the previously stated heroic themes, the scene is a welcomed rest from the ceaseless orchestral agitations that accompanied the inflamed discussion between the two lovers. Its morbid and specious nuances are almost cabalistic in nature, and saturated with troubled harmonies. We are probably justified in saying that this is the only passage in which the quintessence of the subtle and dreamy spirit of the Celts of the Round Table romances appears, rather than the austere and fierce genius of the Charlemagne cycle.

The final act is a poignant masterpiece from beginning to end. After a somber orchestral passage, the commanding rhythm of revolt among the Knights of the Grail eventually climaxes in the fracas of battle, abetted by strident fanfares and reminiscent of Shakespeare's historic melees. The growing restlessness of the music emphasizes clearly the exasperation of the lovers' adventure. Guinevere's invocation of death is musically simple, expressive, personal, and beautiful, a fine page of captivating pathos. It is preceded by a symphonic exordium, a kind of *"lamento funebre"* as penetrating as a *"Dies Irae,"* and a fitting prelude to a passage in which the heroine gives vent to her desperation but retains simultaneously her attitude of impenitence. Antithetical to this, but more touching, is Lancelot's death. Here the music is calmer, interested not in the chills of self-inflicted tragedy but in the warmth of repentance and reconciliation. Due to the soothing tempo of this scene and the gradual elevation in the music, the stage is set now for Arthur's apotheosis. It is a vast peroration, combining a caressingly sonorous orchestra and its occasional off-stage trumpet effects with an invisible chorus, most of the time expanded to eight voices plus five soprano solos. The final theme, at first lulling and ethereal, eventually swells, quickens, and precipitates before being illuminated by Arthur's heroic motif which rises one last time, as radiant as the golden-rose disk of the sun setting slowly in the mystic horizon.

Conclusion

THE life of King Arthur was marked by struggle and disappointment. His epilogical glorification was not so much an assurance as it was a hope for posthumous recognition. *"Tu vivras!"* are among the last words heard by the hero who is so symbolic of Ernest Chausson's artistic life. Yet these words, as we read them slightly over fifty years after the composer's death, have served him but as an imperfect prognostication.

Chausson's premature departure left his reputation as a composer in a precarious position, and many years might have elapsed before his name would have become widely known, had it not been for the loyalty and devotion of his friends—Vincent d'Indy in particular. As we know, the latter completed the unfinished String Quartet, which was first performed on January 27, 1900, at the Société Nationale de Musique. It was D'Indy, too, who first organized an all-Chausson concert at the Schola Cantorum in 1903. The program consisted of *Les Vêpres du Commun des Vierges, Quelques danses,* the *Poème* (performed by Ysaÿe), the String Quartet (by the Parent Quartet), and three *Mélodies* sung by Jeanne Raunay: *Chanson perpétuelle, Les Heures,* and *Serres*

Ernest Chausson

chaudes. Following this, several noteworthy efforts on the part of his friends in France and Belgium were made to foster his works in those countries.

Signal and gratifying was the staging of *Le Roi Arthus* after his death—a performance for which he had worked so hard but unsuccessfully—on November 30, 1903, at the Théâtre de la Monnaie in Brussels. The première had aroused much interest in both the Belgian capital and Paris, so that a scramble for tickets had ensued. That night a glittering audience applauded Chausson's opera, which became a favorite in Brussels.[1] In Paris, however, the reaction to the opera remained indifferent. It was not until 1916 that it was staged, and it was only the third act at that.

Chausson's music made its entry into the United States fairly soon after his death. The first work of his to be performed in this country was probably *Viviane,* played by the Boston Symphony Orchestra on January 31, 1902. Vincent d'Indy introduced the Symphony in B flat during a guest concert by that same orchestra in Philadelphia on December 4, 1905. With the appointment of Pierre Monteux as conductor of the Boston Symphony Orchestra, Chausson's work, along with French music in general, gained an effective champion in the United States. The most memorable of the many brilliant performances of his works under M. Monteux's baton was a rendition of *Soir de fête* from the original score on May 4, 1923; and when the conductor later took

---

[1] As late as September 12, 1909, *Theatra* took a poll of opera-goers, in which the question "Which opera do you wish to see performed at the Monnaie this season?" was answered as follows: *Tristan,* 1273; *Pelléas,* 1216; *Götterdämmerung,* 1211; *Arthus,* 1198. *Theatra,* Vol. II, No. 33 (September 12, 1909), 4.

His Works: Conclusion

charge of the San Francisco Symphony Orchestra, definitive readings continued to delight American audiences.

Yet Lancelot's words to Arthur were never fully realized. Chausson's music has suffered from increasing neglect due to comparisons and historical circumstances which date back to the early 1900's. If it is true, on the one hand, that time then seemed to be in his favor inasmuch as Wagner's music was no longer foremost in the mind of musical audiences—a condition which should have allowed an easier appreciation of Chausson's art—on the other hand, the man whom his art helped prepare, Claude Debussy, representing one of the great climaxes in music history, cast such a wide shadow over his immediate contemporaries that the public eye had, and continues to have, difficulty in discerning the merit of one like Ernest Chausson. Being members of the same generation, certain similarities—such as their sensitive turn of mind and their aristocratic ideals expressed in eminently French terms of highest refinement and subtlety—have contributed to the virtual disappearance of one composer behind the glory of the other. Moreover, the ill-considered utterings of those short-visioned critics who have been unable to distinguish the clearly non-Germanic essence of Chausson's music from Wagner's, or, on occasion, from Franck's, have done their unfair share in placing Chausson in an improper perspective. And finally, this music, which only a short while ago had offended the ears of conservative listeners, seemed now so strongly overshadowed anew, this time by the dazzling innovations of "modern" music, that Pierre Lalo had to state, by way of summary:

Ernest Chausson

This man did not accomplish his destiny . . . Shortly after his death, new musical fashions turned the successive tastes of the public away from his work. Debussyism, Ravelism, Cubism alternately or simultaneously created so much fuss that they easily drowned the already faint echo which comes from the music of a dead man. *Le Roi Arthus,* the only lyrical drama he wrote, which he completed on the eve of his death and which contains admirable scenes, has never been performed [in its entirety] in Paris. His chamber works—his *Concert* for piano, violin, and string quartet, his *Quartet* for piano and strings—are worthy to stand with the works of the most glorious masters of pure music, but are almost never performed. He was one of the best French musicians and he is nearly forgotten.[2]

Although this eclipse is not complete, we feel that during this year, which marks the hundredth anniversary of his birth, a revival of Chausson's works is due. The popularity enjoyed by the Symphony and the *Poème,* and the hazy awareness most music lovers have about the Concert and a number of his *Mélodies,* hardly suffice the man who had the genius to write the Piano Quartet, the *Hymne védique,* the *Shakespeare Songs,* the *Pièce* for 'cello, and the String Quartet. *Viviane, Soir de fête,* the *Chant nuptial,* the Trio, *La Légende de Sainte Cécile,* and the music for Shakespeare's *Tempest,* too, are far better pieces of music than most numbers currently chosen by conductors and musical groups in search of "new" works to add an interest factor to their programs. And this is to say nothing of *Le Roi Arthus* whose third act alone should confer upon it the hitherto forgotten recognition of performance. These compositions still are awaiting the attention which they deserve. If given the proper

[2] *De Rameau à Ravel,* 151.

His Works: Conclusion

opportunity, they will need no extramusical encouragement; they will stand on their own merits. Then, after chance, time will decide, as always. Posterity may seek other offerings, or it may turn, as we hope, to cherish Chausson's music.

For all we know, we may be advancing already towards this desirable end. From here and there one hears of the enthusiasm registered by local groups or isolated individuals over their "discovery" of a Chausson work. Such was the recent excitement at "Tanglewood," (Lenox, Massachusetts) over the String Quartet or at Brandeis University (Waltham, Massachusetts) over the *Chanson perpétuelle*. These are the most tangible indications by which the public will be allowed to pursue an artistic respect for the composer and realize the prophetic words spoken to King Arthur.

If we have heard little of Ernest Chausson, his music possesses, nonetheless—as we have endeavored to illustrate—the qualities which distinguish a fine art. It has craftsmanship and, above all, great inspiration; through them its chances for survival should be secure. But first it must be put through the wear and tear of public awareness, knowledge, and reaction. Then it will invite our appreciation of its consistent musical character, developed not without strain but with commanding elegance. His music will attract us, not by virtue of its novelty but by its unassuming seriousness and sensitiveness of aim. And finally we shall admire, beneath its structure of refinement, the elements of broad humanity, of tenderness and melancholy, which will give it lasting echoes. Let us then conclude with the words of Gustave Samazeuilh, who, in a 1949 broadcast dedicated to Chausson's works, expressed our conviction: "Always turned toward sensitive

Ernest Chausson

expression, anxious to find his way to our hearts rather than dazzle our eyes, to sing rather than to surprise, . . . it is possible that Ernest Chausson's music is likely to appeal but little to advocates of dynamism, atonality, dodecaphony, or even to certain romantics who prefer more incisive notations. Nevertheless, after half a century, it has not lost its sway over those who still like poetry, loftiness of thought, the cult of grandeur, and who, behind the notes which are only the exterior garb of music, look for the soul which they reveal."

Bibliography

Aubry, Georges Jean. *French Music of Today*. Translated by Edwin Evans. London, K. Paul, Trench, Trubner, and Co., 1926.

Bellaigue, Camille. *Paroles et musiques*. Paris, Perrin and Co., 1925.

Bouchor, Maurice. *"Le Langage et l'Esprit,"* *Revue Musicale,* Vol. I, No. 2 (December 1, 1925), 180–90.

Bréville, Pierre de. "Ernest Chausson," *Mercure de France,* Vol. XXXI (September, 1899), 687–94.

Bruneau, Alfred. *La Musique française*. Paris, E. Fasquelle Co., 1901.

Calvocoressi, M-D. *"A la Mémoire d'Ernest Chausson,"* *l'Art Moderne,* Vol. XXIII (May 24, 1903), 189–90.

Carraud, Gaston. "Ernest Chausson," *Le Menestrel,* Vol. LXXXII (April 2, 1920), 137–39.

Chausson, Ernest. *"Fervaal,"* *Mercure de France,* Vol. XXII (April, 1897), 128–36.

——. "César Franck," *Le Passant,* 1891.

Cooper, Martin. *French Music*. London, New York, Oxford University Press, 1951.

Deledicque, Michel Raux. *Albéniz, su vida inquieta y ardorosa*. Buenos Aires, Ediciones Peuser, 1950.

Dubois, Anthony. "Ernest Chausson," *Guide Musical,* Vol. XLV (July 2, 1899), 516–17.

Ernest Chausson

Du Bos, Charles. *"Chausson et la Consolation par le Coeur,"* *Revue Musicale,* December 1, 1925, 99–107.

Gauthier-Villars, Henri (Willy). *La Colle aux Quintes.* Paris, H. Simonis Empis, 1899.

———. *Garçon, l'Audition!* Paris, H. Simonis Empis, 1901.

Grove, George. "Ernest Chausson," *Grove's Dictionary of Music and Musicians.* 2 vols. London, Macmillan and Co.; New York, St. Martin's Press, 1954.

Hallays, André. *"Le Roi Arthus,"* *Revue de Paris,* Vol. VI (December 15, 1903), 846–58.

Hervey, Arthur. *French Music in the Nineteenth Century.* London, G. Richards; New York, E. P. Dutton and Co., 1903.

Hoerée, Arthur. *"Chausson et la Musique française,"* *Revue Musicale,* December 1, 1925, 191–206.

Indy, Vincent d'. "Ernest Chausson," *La Tribune de Saint-Gervais,* September, 1899.

———. "Ernest Chausson," *Cobbett's Cyclopedic Survey of Chamber Music.* 2 vols. London, Oxford University Press, 1929–30.

Lalo, Pierre. *De Rameau à Ravel.* Paris, A. Michel, 1947.

Le Flem, Paul. *"Chausson et la Musique pure,"* *Euterpe,* No. 8 (September, 1949), 114–25.

Lindelaub, Th. "Ernest Chausson," *Revue Eolienne,* August, 1899.

Lockspeiser, Edward. *Debussy.* London, J. M. Dent and Sons; New York, E. P. Dutton and Co., 1936.

———. "The French Song in the Nineteenth Century," *The Musical Quarterly,* Vol. XXVI (1940), 192–99.

McKinney, Howard, and W. R. Anderson. *Music in History.* New York, Cincinnati, American Book Co., 1940.

Mason, Daniel G. *Contemporary Composers.* New York, Macmillan Co., 1929.

Masson, Paul-Marie. *"Chausson et le Symbolisme,"* *La Dépêche,* March 31, 1936. (This article, from a newspaper which no longer exists, was found by the authors in the Chausson family scrapbook.)

Bibliography

Mauclair, Camille. *La Religion de la Musique.* Paris, Fischbacher, 1909.

———. *"Souvenirs sur Ernest Chausson,"* La Vogue, Vol. III (August 15, 1899), 73–82.

———. *"Le Lied français contemporain,"* Musica, Vol. VII, No. 74 (November, 1908), 163–64.

———. *Histoire de la Musique européenne, 1850–1914.* Paris, Fischbacher, 1914.

Maus, Madeleine-Octave. *Trente années de lutte pour l'Art* (1884–1914). Brussels, Libraire l'Oiseau Bleu, 1926.

Maus, Octave. "Ernest Chausson," *l'Art Moderne,* Vol. XIX (June 18, 1899), 205–207.

———. "Ernest Chausson," *Courrier Musical,* November 26, 1899.

Oulmont, Charles. *"Deux amis, Claude Debussy et Ernest Chausson. Documents inédits,"* Mercure de France, Vol. CCLVI (December 1, 1934), 248–69.

———. *Musique de l'Amour* (on Ernest Chausson and *"la bande à Franck"*). 2 vols. Paris, Desclée, de Brouwer and Co., 1935.

Remacle, Adrien. *"Mélodies et Mélodistes,"* La Mode Pratique, October, 1895.

Revue Belge de Musicologie, III, Part II (1949).

Revue Musicale, Vol. I, No. 2 (December 1, 1925). This is a special issue devoted to Ernest Chausson, containing unpublished correspondence and articles by Charles Du Bos, Maurice Bouchor, Arthur Hoerée, and Gustave Samazeuilh.

Reynaud, Louis. *L'influence allemande en France au XVIIIe et XIXe siècle.* Paris, Hachette Co., 1922.

Risvaëg, Stéphane. *"La Symphonie en si bémol d'Ernest Chausson,"* Guide Musical, Vol. XLV (April 9, 1899), 345–46.

Rolland, Romain. *Essays on Music.* New York, Crown Co., 1948.

Samazeuilh, Gustave. *"Ernest Chausson et le 'Roi Arthus,'"* Revue Musicale, Vol. III (December 15, 1903), 609–705.

———. "Ernest Chausson," *Revue Musicale* (December 1, 1925), 109–15.

Ernest Chausson

———. "Ernest Chausson," *Euterpe,* No. 7 (July, 1949), 110–23.

Séré, Octave. *Musiciens français d'aujourd'hui.* Paris, *Mercure de France,* 1911.

Servières, Georges. *"Lieder français, Ernest Chausson,"* Guide *Musical,* Vol. XLIII (December 19, 1897), 843–46.

Sorabji, Kaikhosru Shapurji. *Mi Contra Fa: The Immoralisings of a Machiavellian Musician.* London, Porcupine Press, 1947.

Tiersot, Julien. "Ernest Chausson," *Guide Musical,* Vol. XLV (June 25, 1899), 503–504.

———. *Un demi-siècle de musique française* (1870–1919). Paris, F. Alcan, 1918.

Vallas, Léon. *Les Idées de Claude Debussy.* London, Oxford University Press, 1929.

———. *Claude Debussy.* Translated by Maire and Grace O'Brien. London, Oxford University Press, 1933.

———. *Vincent d'Indy.* 2 vols. Paris, A. Michel, 1946.

"Verlaine," *Columbia Dictionary of Modern European Literature.* New York, New York, Columbia University Press, 1947.

Verlaine, Paul Marie. *Romances sans paroles.* Paris, G. Crès and Co., 1923.

List of Ernest Chausson's Compositions

I. *Mélodies* and other compositions
for voice and accompaniment

A. Voice and Piano

Op. 2: *Sept mélodies*

    1. *Nanny* (Leconte de Lisle, *"Poèmes antiques"*);
      1879–80

    2. *Le Charme* (Armand Silvestre, *"Chanson des Heures"*);
      Oct. 1879

    3. *Les Papillons* (Théophile Gautier)

    4. *La dernière feuille* (Théophile Gautier);
      1880

    5. *Sérénade italienne* (Paul Bourget)

    6. *Hébé* (Ackermann)
      Dedicated to Mlle Eva Callimaki-Catargi

    7. *Le Colibri* (Leconte de Lisle)
      Dedicated to Lady Harbord
      1882 (Hamelle)

Op. 8: *Quatre mélodies* (Maurice Bouchor)

    1. Nocturne
      Cannes, Feb., 1886

2. *Amour d'antan*
   Etampes, Aug., 1882
3. *Printemps triste*
   Pressagny l'Orgueilleux, Sept. 23, 1883
4. *Nos souvenirs*
   Crémault, July, 1888
   (Rouart-Lerolle)

Op. 13: *Quatre mélodies*
   1. *Apaisement* (Paul Verlaine)
      1885
      Dedicated to C. Benoît
   2. *Sérénade* (Jean Lahor)
      1887
      Dedicated to Maurice Bagès de Trigny
   3. *l'Aveu* (Villiers de l'Isle-Adam)
      1887
      Dedicated to Paul Poujaud
   4. *La Cigale* (Leconte de Lisle)
      July 12, 1887
      Dedicated to Mlle Marie Escudier
      (Hamelle)

Op. 14: *La Caravane* (Théophile Gautier)
      1887
      Dedicated to Ernest Van Dyck
      (Hamelle)

Op. 17: *Chansons de Miarka* (Jean Richepin)
   1. *Les Morts*
   2. *La Pluie*
      1888
      Both dedicated to Mlle Fanny Lépine
      (Bornemann)

Op. 24: *Serres chaudes* (Maurice Maeterlinck)
   1. *Serre chaude*
      Paris, March 19, 1896

Compositions

2. *Serre d'Ennui*
Luzancy, July 7, 1893
3. *Lassitude*
Luzancy, June 30, 1893
4. *Fauves las*
Paris, Feb. 27, 1896
5. *Oraison*
Florence, Feb., 1895; Paris, Feb. 27, 1896
Dedicated to Mlle Thérèse Roger
(Rouart-Lerolle)

Op. 27: *Trois lieder* (Camille Mauclair)
1. *Les Heures*
Bas Bel Air, Sept., 1896
Dedicated to Mme B. Rouquairol
2. Ballade
Paris, March, 1896
Dedicated to Mme Maurice Sulzbach
3. *Les Couronnes*
Bas Bel Air, Sept., 1896
Dedicated to Mme Maurice Denis
(Rouart-Lerolle)

Op. 28: *Chansons de Shakespeare* (translations by Maurice Bouchor)
1. *Chanson de clown* (*Twelfth Night*)
Cuincy, May, 1890
2. *Chanson d'amour* (*Measure for Measure*)
Civray, July, 1891
3. *Chanson d'Ophélie* (*Hamlet*)
Paris, Dec. 4, 1896
4. See under I, C ("Chorus and Duets")
1897 (Rouart-Lerolle)

Op. 33: *Pour un Arbre de Noël*
About 1898
Unpublished

Ernest Chausson

Op. 34: *Deux poèmes* (Paul Verlaine)

    1. *La Chanson bien douce*
    June, 1898
    Dedicated to Etiennette Chausson
    (Rouart-Lerolle)

    2. *Le Chevalier Malheur*
    1898
    1925 (*Revue Musicale*)

Op. 36: *Deux mélodies*

    1. *Cantique à l'Épouse* (Albert Jounet)
    Bois St. Martin, June 23, 1898

    2. *Dans la Forêt du Charme et de l'Enchantement*
    (Jean Moréas)
    Oct., 1898
    Dedicated to Mme Jeanne Remacle
    (Rouart-Lerolle)

Unpublished

W* 41: *Lilas, vos frissons sous le Ciel* (Maurice Bouchor, "Dans la Forêt")
    1878

W 42: *Le petit sentier* (Maurice Bouchor)
    1878

W 43: *l'Albatros* (Baudelaire, *"Les Fleurs du Mal"*)
    For contralto and piano
    1879

W 44: *Le Rideau de ma voisine* (Alfred de Musset)
    March 1879

* Works marked "W" are unpublished scores which have no opus number; most of these can be found in the Paris Conservatory or in the Bibliothèque Nationale in Paris. As far as possible these works are numbered in approximate chronological order, beginning with "W 40," the opus number which would follow Chausson's last published work.

Compositions

W 55: *Nous nous aimerons* (author not indicated)
1882

W 57: *Le Mort maudit* (Jean Richepin)
1884

B. Voice and Orchestra

Op. 19: *Poème de l'Amour et de la Mer* (Maurice Bouchor)
1. *La Fleur des Eaux*
2. Interlude
3. *La Mort de l'Amour*
(The final song has been published separately as *"Le Temps des Lilas"*; it was composed in Bellevue, in 1886)
1882–92
Dedicated to Henri Duparc
First performance: February 21, 1893, in Brussels; sung by Désiré Demest, with Chausson playing the piano. (Rouart-Lerolle)

Op. 37: *Chanson perpétuelle* (Charles Cros)
Paris, Dec. 17, 1898
Dedicated to Mme Jeanne Raunay
First performance: January 29, 1899, in Le Havre; sung by Mme Jeanne Raunay.
(Durand)

Unpublished

W 49: *Esmeralda* (Victor Hugo; Act IV, sc. 1)
1880

C. Chorus and Duets

Op. 9: *Hymne védique* (Leconte de Lisle)
Chorus of four mixed voices with orchestral accompaniment

Ernest Chausson

1886
Dedicated to César Franck
(Hamelle)

Op. 11: *Deux duos*
1. *La Nuit* (Th. de Banville)
   Dedicated to Mme I. Allin
2. *Le Réveil* (Balzac)
   Dedicated to Mme Pauline Roger
   1883
   (Hamelle)

Op. 15: *Chant nuptial* (Leconte de Lisle)
For chorus of four women's voices
About 1887
(Hamelle)

Op. 28: *Chansons de Shakespeare* (translations by Maurice Bouchor)
4. *Chant funèbre* (*Much Ado about Nothing*)
   For women's choir, four voices; orchestral accompaniment by Vincent d'Indy
   1897
   (Rouart-Lerolle)

Op. 29: Ballata (after Dante)
For choir of four voices, without accompaniment
1897

Unpublished

W 40: *Hylas* (Leconte de Lisle, *"Poèmes antiques"*)
For soli, chorus, and orchestra; pre-orchestral version
Fragment
No date

W 47: *La Veuve du Roi basque*
Ballade for orchestra, soli, and choirs
Marked Op. 3

Compositions

Zurich, 1879
Reduction (called *Suite basque* for orchestra) for piano (four hands) by Charles Bordes (published by Bornemann)

W 51: *Hymne à la Nature* (Armand Sylvestre)
Choir of four voices with orchestral accompaniment
1881

W 53: *l'Arabe* (author not indicated)
For men's choir with tenor solo and orchestra (preorchestral version)
Presented for *Prix de Rome* contest
May 13, 1881

W 56: *Chanson de noces dans les Bois* (imitated from a Lithuanian song by André Theuriet)
For duet (two soprani) and piano
(Added in pencil: "Op. 11, No. 3," but only two songs published under that opus number)
1883

II. Dramatic and Incidental Music

no op. *Jeanne d'Arc* (author not indicated)
number Lyrical scene for soli and women's chorus
About 1880
(Rouart-Lerolle)

Op. 4: *Les Caprices de Marianne* (Lyrical comedy after Alfred de Musset)
1880–82
Entr'acte (*"La Mort de Coelio"*) performed at Société Nationale on April 18, 1885
Unpublished

Op. 7: *Hélène* (Lyrical drama in two acts after Leconte de Lisle)
Two scenes performed at Société Nationale on May 14,

Ernest Chausson

1887, and January 21, 1888
Unpublished except:
1. Women's chorus with orchestra
2. *Le Jugement de Pâris*
    For baritone and orchestra
    (Rouart-Lerolle)

Op. 18: *La Tempête* (Incidental music for Shakespeare's comedy, translated by Maurice Bouchor)
For small orchestra (one flute, one violin, one harp, one celeste)
1. *Chant d'Ariel*
2. *Air de danse*
3. Duet between Juno and Ceres
4. *Danse rustique*
5. *Chanson d'Ariel*
1888
Dedicated to Henri Signoret
First performance: December, 1888, at the Petit Théâtre des Marionettes
(Bornemann)

Op. 22: *La Légende de Sainte-Cécile* (Music for the drama by Maurice Bouchor)
For soli, women's choir, and small orchestra
1892
Dedicated to Raymond Bonheur
First performance: January 25, 1892, at the Petit Théâtre des Marionettes
(Joubert)

Unpublished

W 59: *Les Oiseaux* (Incidental music for Aristophanes' comedy)
For flute and harp
1889

Compositions

III. Religious Music

Op. 6: *Deux motets* for voice, violin, and organ
    1. *Deus Abraham*
    2. *Ave Verum*
    1883
    (Hamelle)

Op. 12: *Trois motets* for four mixed voices, cello, harp, and
    organ
    1. *Ave Maria*
    2. *Tota pulchra es*
    3. *Ave maris stella*
    1886
    Unpublished except no. 2 (Rouart-Lerolle)

Op. 16: *Trois motets*
    1. *Lauda Sion Salvatorem*
      1888
    2. *Benedictus*
      1890
    3. *Pater Noster*
      1891
    Unpublished except no. 3 (Rouart-Lerolle)

Op. 31: *Les Vêpres du Commun des Vierges*
    1897
    Edition Mutuelle

    Unpublished

W 45: *O Salutons,* motet for bass and organ (or piano)
    1879

Ernest Chausson

IV. Chamber Music
and Music for Solo Instruments

Op. 1: *Cinq fantaisies pour piano* (Five Fantasies for piano)
(two hands); destroyed
About 1879
Dedicated to Monsieur Leopoldo Cesare
(Durand)

Op. 3: Trio in G minor for piano, violin, and cello
1881
First performance: April 8, 1882, with André Messager,
Rémy, and Delsart
1919 (Rouart-Lerolle)

Op. 21: Concert in D Major for piano, violin, and string quartet
1889–91
Dedicated to Eugène Ysaÿe
First performance: March 4, 1892, in Brussels; with
Auguste Pierret, Eugène Ysaÿe, and the Crickboom
Quartet (Crickboom, Birmasz, Van Hout, Jacob)
(Rouart-Lerolle)

Op. 26: *Quelques danses* (A Few Dances) for piano (two hands)
1. *Dédicace*
2. Sarabande
3. Pavane
4. *Forlane*
June–July, 1896
Dedicated to Mme Robert de Bonnières
(Rouart-Lerolle)

Op. 30: Quartet in A Major for piano, violin, viola, and cello
1897
Dedicated to Auguste Pierret
First performance: April 2, 1898, at the Société Na-

Compositions

tionale; with Auguste Pierret, Armand Parent, Denayer, and Baretti
1917 (Rouart-Lerolle)

Op. 35: Quartet (unfinished) in C minor for two violins, viola, and cello (completed by Vincent d'Indy)
1899
Dedicated to Mathieu Crickboom
First performance: January 27, 1900, at the Société Nationale; with Armand Parent, Lammers, Denayer, Baretti
(Durand)

Op. 38: *Paysage* (Landscape) for piano (two hands)
1895
Dedicated to Mlle Christine Lerolle
(Rouart-Lerolle)

Op. 39: *Pièce* for cello (or viola) and piano
1897
Dedicated to J. Gaillard
1917 (Rouart-Lerolle)

Unpublished

W 46: Sonatina in D minor for piano (four hands)
Marked Op. 2
1879

W 48: Sonata in F minor for piano
1879–80

W 50: Eleven Fugues for four voices on themes by Bach, Franck, Hesse, Massenet, and Saint-Saëns
1880–81

W 52: Andante and Allegro for clarinet, with piano accompaniment
April 28, 1881

Ernest Chausson

W 54: *Fugue à quatre voix sur un Thème de Saint-Saëns*
(Fugue for Four Voices on a Theme by Saint-Saëns)
1881
Presented for *Prix de Rome* contest

W 58: Marche militaire for piano
1884

V. Orchestral Music

Op. 5: *Viviane* (Symphonic poem based on a legend of the
Round Table)
1882
Dedicated to Mlle Jeanne Escudier
First performance: March 31, 1883, at the Société Na-
tionale (Salle Erard), Colonne conducting
First performance of revised version: January 29, 1888,
at Concert Lamoureux
First performance in the United States: January 31,
1902, by Boston Symphony
(Bornemann)

Op. 10: *Solitude dans les Bois* (Solitude in the Woods) for orchestra (later destroyed)
1886
First performance: December 12, 1886, at Eden Theater
in Paris

Op. 20: Symphony in B flat Major
1889–90
Dedicated to Henry Lerolle
First performance: April 18, 1891, at the Société Na-
tionale, Chausson conducting
First major performance: May 13, 1897, at Cirque
d'Hiver, by Berlin Philharmonic Orchestra, Arthur
Nikisch conducting
First performance in the United States: December 4,

Compositions

1905, in Philadelphia, by Boston Symphony, Vincent d'Indy conducting
(Rouart-Lerolle)

Op. 25: *Poème* for violin and orchestra
1896
Dedicated to Eugène Ysaÿe
First performance: October, 1896, at party of artists in Spain; soloist: Ysaÿe
First public performance: December, 1896, at Concert du Conservatoire in Nancy; soloist: Ysaÿe
First Paris performance: April 4, 1897, at Concert Colonne; soloist: Ysaÿe
(Breitkopf & Haertel)

Op. 32: *Soir de fête* (Holiday Evening) for orchestra
January 31, 1898, at San Domenico di Fiesole
Dedicated to Edouard Colonne
First performance: March 13, 1898, at Concert Colonne
First performance in the United States: May 4, 1923, by Boston Symphony, Pierre Monteux conducting
Unpublished

W 60: Symphony No. 2 (sketch of the opening)
1899

VI. Operatic Music

Op. 23: *Le Roi Arthus* (Lyrical drama in 3 acts and 6 scenes; libretto by Chausson)
1886–95
First performance: November 30, 1903, at the Théâtre de la Monnaie in Brussels; with Mme Paquot-d'Assy (Genièvre), M. Albers (Arthus), M. Dalmorès (Lancelot), M. François (Mordred), M. Forgeur (Lyonnel), M. Vallier (Allan), and M. Cotreuil (Merlin); conductor: Sylvain Dupuis
(Choudens)

225

Ernest Chausson

VII. Transcriptions by Chausson

W 61: Lully: *Atys* (Prelude, aria, and sleeping scene from
         Act III)
         Reconstitution of the orchestra
W 62: Rameau: *Les Indes galantes* ("Adoration of the sun"—
         solo and chorus)
         Reconstitution of the orchestra
W 63: Beethoven: String Quartets
                      no. 1 (adagio)
                            2 (scherzo)
                            9 (andante)
                           13 (cavatina)
                           15 (*canzone di ringraziamento;*
                                andante)
                           17 (lento)

VIII. Literature by Chausson

"César Franck," *Le Passant,* 1891
"Fervaal," Mercure de France, April 1897
Le Roi Arthus; libretto for his opera. 1886–95
La Vie est un Songe; libretto for a projected opera.
1899

(NOTE: The works of Chausson which are published by Rouart-Lerolle can
be obtained in the United States through: Salabert Inc., 1 East 57th St.,
New York, N.Y.)

Index

Ernest Chausson

Ballata (Opus 29): 179, 182, 218
Balzac, Honoré de: 76, 131
Banville, Théodore de: 131
Baudelaire, Charles: 4
Beethoven, Ludwig van: 14, 22, 112, 147
Benedictus (Opus 16, No. 2): 221
Benoît, Camille: 18n., 33, 35, 105
Berlin Philharmonic Orchestra: 85, 89
Berlioz, Hector: 4, 19
Besnard, Albert: 34, 105
Bizet, Georges: 14, 20–21, 194
Bonheur, Raymond: 35, 37, 37n., 55, 60, 105
Bonnat, Joseph-Léon: 36
Bordes, Charles: 17, 18n., 35, 47, 103, 107, 117
Boris Godunov (Moussorgsky): 60
Boston Symphony Orchestra: 204
Botticelli, Sandro: 33, 51
Bouchor, Maurice: 35, 38, 40, 51, 52, 56, 74, 98, 122, 123, 128, 183
Bouguereau, Adolphe: 50
Brahms, Johannes: 118
Breitkopf, (?), publisher: 85
Bréville, Pierre de: 17, 18n., 40, 44, 47, 54, 76, 103, 105, 107
Bruneau, Alfred: 15, 22n., 92, 105
Bussine, Romain: 14
Buxtehude, Dietrich: 174

Cahn, Albert: 96
Calderón de la Barca, Pedro: 100, 103
Cantique à l'Epouse (Opus 36, No. 1): 10n., 100, 130–31, 216
Caprices de Marianne, Les (Opus 4): 179n., 219
Caravane, La (Opus 14): 38, 40, 118, 127–28, 214
Carmen (Bizet): 20–21, 194
Carrière, Eugène: 34, 105
Castillon, Alexis de: 18n., 103, 146
Catalonia (Albéniz): 94

Index

Cavalleria Rusticana (Mascagni): 96

Chabrier, Emmanuel: 15, 20, 35, 104

Chanson bien douce, La (Opus 34, No. 1): 125–26, 216

Chanson d'amour (Opus 28, No. 2): 128–29, 215

Chanson de Clown (Opus 28, No. 1): 128, 215

Chanson d'Ophélie (Opus 28, No. 3): 129, 215

Chanson perpétuelle (Opus 37): 10n., 69n., 74, 75, 100, 101, 107, 129–30, 173, 203, 207, 217

Chansons de Miarka (Opus 17): 38, 132–33, 214

Chansons de Shakespeare (Opus 28): 75, 128–29, 206, 215, 218

Chant funèbre (Opus 28, No. 4): 129, 218

Chant nuptial (Opus 15): 179, 182, 206, 218

Charme, Le (Opus 2, No. 2): 10, 131, 213

Charpentier, Alexandre-Louis-Marie (sculptor): 105

Charpentier, Gustave: 90

Chausson, Ernest: 15, 17, 19, 47, 103; parents, 5; correct birth date, 5n.; influence of his tutor, 6; his melancholy, 6, 34, 75–77, 111, 195; influence of Mme de Rayssac, 6ff.; studies law, 7; his "pudeur," 8, 30–31, 79–80, 111, 113, 133; his sense of humor, 8–9, 77–78; planned works not materialized, 9, 26, 32–33, 100, 102–103, 149n.; his travels, 9, 11, 29, 41, 50–51, 61, 63, 84, 86, 91, 101; decides to devote himself to music, 9; concern with form, 9–10, 29, 31, 55, 125, 127, 142, 165; premonition of death, 10, 31–32, 129, 147; enrolls in Conservatory, 10; first compositions, 10; destroys his Opus 1, 10; opinion of Wagner, 11, 27–28, 38, 67, 72–73, 193–95; decides to study with Franck, 11; friendship with Chabrier, 20; friendship with Fauré, 21, 46; on Franck, 22, 48–49, 95; enters Prix de Rome competition, 22–23; difficulties in composing, 23, 26–27, 38–39, 41–46, 71–72, 73, 90, 104; on dilettantism, 23, 27; emotional make-up, 23–24, 79–80; attitude towards nature, 24, 29, 30, 33, 160; marriage, 25, children, 25; influence of wife, 25–26; composing habits, 26, 41, 103, 140; military service, 26; and romanticism, 29–31, 66; lyricism, 31, 127, 144, 173, 177, 180–81, 195, 200; on death, 31–32; his inspirations, 32–33, 83, 97, 113, 165, 176; on descrip-

229

Index

kov's *Antar,* 96; suggestiveness of his music, 97–98, 126, 159; his conception of *Soir de fête,* 99, performance of *Viviane* in Moscow, 101; on Georgette Leblanc, 102; his last days, 102–104; as librettist, 103, 198–99; his death, 104, 107; his funeral, 105; posthumous tributes by Pierre Louÿs, Ysaÿe, and Willy, 105 ff.; his *Mélodies,* 106, 115, 117–34, 176, 206, 213–17; position in music history, 111, 112, 115; his style, 112, 119, 174; demands of his music on performers, 112, 156, 157; his individuality, 112–13, 133–34, 174; his sensitivity, 113, 115, 178, 195; effect of his music on listener, 114, 115, 134, 158, 208; impersonalism of his music, 115, 135, 157; conflicts in his music, 115–16; as representative of his generation, 116; harmony in his music, 120, 121, 124, 127, 128, 129, 131, 136, 139, 155, 156, 157, 163, 164, 174, 177, 180, 181, 182, 183, 195, 199, 201; rhythm in his music, 120, 122, 124, 126, 127, 130, 131, 141, 142, 147, 148, 149, 150, 151, 152, 160, 162, 181, 182, 200; chromaticism and modulations in his music, 120, 121, 124, 126, 128, 130, 132–33, 141, 150, 151, 156, 160, 162–64, 168, 171, 172, 180, 184–86, 199; as musical interpreter of poems, 121–22, 125–26, 134, 182, 183, 199; his melodic line, 121–22, 176–77, 195; religious music, 135–39, 175–76, 180, 200, 221; chamber music, 140–58, 222–24; use of cyclic themes, 142, 148, 151–53, 165, 174; composing technique, 143–45; orchestral music, 159–78, 224–25; orchestration, 159–60, 162, 165, 183, 184, 195–96, 199, 201; search for an ideal, 175–76, 191–92; mysticism, 175–76; dramatic, choral, and incidental music, 179–86, 219–20; his opera, 187–202, 225; on effort, 191–92; identified with hero of his opera, 192; on D'Indy's *Fervaal,* 193–95; on personality of artist, 194; fate of his music after death, 203–206; his music performed in the United States, 204; compared to Debussy, 205; neglected works worthy of performance, 206; "discovery" of, by American audiences, 207; homage to, by Samazeuilh, 207–208; unpublished works without opus number, 216–17, 218–19, 220, 221, 223–24, 225; transcriptions by, 226; literature by, 226

Chausson, Mme Ernest: 25, 57, 67, 84, 91–92, 108

Index

Chausson's Concert, 146–47; finishes Chausson's String Quartet, 155; inventor of term "cyclic," 165; Chausson on *Fervaal,* 193–95; arranges all-Chausson concert, 203; conducts Chausson's Symphony in United States, 204
Iphigénie en Aulide (Gluck): 11

Jardin aux Lilas (Tudor): 98
Jeanne d'Arc (no opus number): 179n., 219
Joncières, (?), music critic: 87
Jounet, Albert: 131

Koechlin, Charles: 35, 105
Kufferath, Maurice: 102

Lalo, Edouard: 15, 194
Lalo, Pierre: 105, 200, 205–206
Laloy, Louis: 100
Lamartine, Alphonse: 3
Lamoureux, Charles: 15, 81
Lassitude (Opus 24, No. 3): 121, 215
Lauda Sion Salvatorem (Opus 16, No. 1): 139, 221
La Villemarqué, Théodore Hersart: 161
Lazzari, Sylvio: 18n., 35, 105
Leblanc, Georgette: 81, 102
Légende de Sainte-Cécile, La (Opus 22): 37n., 51–52, 71, 81, 102, 107, 135, 139, 179, 184–86, 206, 220
Lekeu, Guillaume: 15, 18n., 103, 117, 147
Lenoir, Alfred: 25, 105
Lerolle, Guillaume: 5n.
Lerolle, Henry: 5n., 25, 34, 37n., 42, 46, 59, 60, 79n.
Lisle, Leconte de: 33, 74, 122, 127, 179 182, 183
Lohengrin (Wagner): 15, 16
Louÿs, Pierre: 105, 107

Madame Bovary (Flaubert): 4

235

Index

Oiseaux, Les (no opus number): 179n., 220
Oraison (Opus 24, No. 5): 121, 215
Oulmont, Charles: 115
Ouverture de Shéhérazade (Ravel): 94

Papillons, Les (Opus 2, No. 3): 10, 120, 131, 213
Parent, Armand: 35, 223
Parsifal (Wagner): 37n.
Pascal, Blaise: 24, 31
Pasdeloup, Jules (Etienne): 15
Pater Noster (Opus 16, No. 3): 136, 221
Paysage (Opus 38): 74, 82, 156, 157, 223
Pelléas et Mélisande (Debussy): 35, 62, 64, 69, 195, 204n.
Pepita Jiménez (Albéniz): 91
Piano Quartet (Opus 30): 74, 90, 93–94, 106, 112, 115, 140, 148–54, 156, 158, 173, 206, 222–23
Pièce for cello and piano (Opus 39): 93, 156, 158, 206, 223
Pierret, Auguste: 54, 94, 222
Pluie, La (Opus 17, No. 2): 133, 214
Poe, Edgar A.: 55
Poème for violin and orchestra (Opus 25): 74, 83–88, 98, 105–106, 115, 159, 160, 173, 176–78, 180, 203, 206, 225
Poème de l'Amour et de la Mer (Opus 19): 38, 56–58, 71, 74, 107, 123, 158, 160, 217
Pougin, Arthur: 50
Poujaud, Paul: 26, 35, 46, 72, 82, 105, 191
Poulenc, Francis: 117
Pour un arbre de Noël (Opus 33): 215
Printemps triste (Opus 8, No. 3): 123, 214
Prix de Rome: 22n.
Prophète, Le (Meyerbeer): 10
Proses lyriques (Debussy): 65, 69
Proust, Marcel: 35
Pugno, Raoul: 105

237

Ernest Chausson

Quartet (Debussy): 68, 69
Quartet, Piano (Opus 30): *see* Piano Quartet
Quartet, String (Opus 35): *see* String Quartet
Quelques danses (Opus 26): 84, 156–57, 203, 222

Racine, Jean: 194
Raphael, Sanzio: 32, 51
Raunay, Mme Jeanne: 101, 107, 203, 217
Ravel, Maurice: 15, 37, 94
Rayssac, Mme de: 6, 7, 8, 9, 22, 24, 30
Rayssac, Saint-Cyr de: 6
Redon, Odilon: 34, 38, 105
Régnier, Henri de: 35, 105
Renoir, Auguste: 34
Réveil, Le (Opus 11, No. 2): 131–32, 218
Richepin, Jean: 38, 132
Rimbaud, Arthur: 69, 70
Rimski-Korsakov, Nikolai: 96
Rodin, Auguste: 34–35, 105
Roi Arthus, Le (Opus 23): 59, 62, 70, 76, 81, 82, 103, 106, 107, 146,
    160, 179, 180, 206, 225; first draft of libretto, 34; difficulties in
    work on, 38, 60, 65, 71–72; work on third act, 67; attempts to
    get performance of, 91–93, 101–102; summary of libretto, 187–
    90; comparison with *Tristan,* 195–97; quality of libretto, 198;
    première of, 204; popularity of, in Brussels, 204n., cast of *pre-
    mière,* 225
Rolland, Romain: 15, 75n.
Rondel (Debussy): 69n.
Ronsard, Pierre de: 123
Ropartz, Guy: 17, 18n., 35, 47, 103, 107, 117
Rousseau, Jean-Jacques: 112
Roussel, Albert: 117
Rusinol, Santiago: 84

Saint-Saëns, Camille: 14, 15, 20, 95, 194

238

Index

Salvayre, G.: 87–88, 195
Samazeuilh, Gustave: *ix,* 35, 37, 96n., 104, 105, 207
San Francisco Symphony Orchestra: 205
Satie, Eric: 35
Schola Cantorum: 17n., 18n.
Schopenhauer, Arthur: 24, 75
Schubert, Franz: 10, 19, 118, 135
Schumann, Robert: 9, 118
Sérénade (Opus 13, No. 2): 120, 214
Sérénade italienne (Opus 2, No. 5): 120, 213
Serre chaude (Opus 24, No. 1): 119, 121, 214
Serre d'ennui (Opus 24, No. 2): 121, 215
Serres, Louis de: 105, 107
Serres chaudes (Opus 24): 62, 71, 75, 84, 119–22, 203–204, 214–15
Shakespeare: 40, 122, 128–29, 201
Shakespeare Songs: see Chansons de Shakespeare
Siegfried (Wagner): 75
Société des Chanteurs de Saint-Gervais: 18n.
Société Nationale de Musique: 14–15, 20, 24, 25, 47, 57, 67, 78, 81, 87, 94, 203
Soir de fête (Opus 32): 74, 94, 96, 98–100, 106, 159, 161–64, 176, 204, 206, 225
Solitude dans les Bois (Opus 10): 33–34, 41, 95, 96, 98, 161, 224
Song of Roland: 45
Sorabji, Kaikhosru S.: 143, 177
Stendhal: 76
Strauss, Johann: 156
String Quartet (Opus 35): 74, 100, 102, 103, 104, 106, 140, 154–56, 203, 206, 207, 223
Symphony in B flat Major (Opus 20): 38, 41–49, 54, 71, 72, 73, 81, 84, 89–90, 94, 98, 106, 115, 146, 156, 159, 164–76, 193, 204, 206, 224–25

Tannhäuser (Wagner): 15, 16
Tempête, La (Opus 18): 40, 54, 101, 107, 179, 183–84, 206, 220

Index

Ernest Chausson

has been composed in types which are unequivocally French. That used for the text is Linotype *Granjon,* designed by the English printer, George W. Jones, in 1924, and named in honor of a famous French type designer, Jean Granjon. While it is not a direct copy of an earlier type, it is extremely close in flavor and detail to the sixteenth-century types of Claude Garamond. The type used on the title page and for the chapter openings is called *Garamond,* though recent analysis has shown that it is not a copy (which it was thought to be) of any of Garamond's types, but rather of those cut by Jean Jannon about 1620. All this would suggest that perhaps Granjon should be called Garamond, and Garamond Jannon. But aside from confusions of names and lineage, the types remain distinctly French and reveal their Gallic heritage; they are graceful, dignified, and utilitarian. In these respects, they are eminently suitable for this book on Ernest Chausson.

University of Oklahoma Press : Norman

Date Due